THE INSPIRATION
AND
TESTING GROUND

Swell lines pour onto Gold Coast sand — the inspiration and testing ground
for the revolutionary triple-stitched Billabong boardshort, developed by a
young surfer and his wife in 1973.

PHOTO BY ANDREW SHIELD

2

ANDY

ANDY IRONS SAYS: "Sit on the ledge. When the wave comes don't paddle out to the horizon, sit and wait. Let it come to you. Paddle down the face as fast as you can. Watch the nose of your board. Pray." Andy Irons, Teahupo'o, Tahiti. (The amorphous blob floating up the face of the wave is Hawaiian Shane Dorian, a well-known lover of big waves. In his paw he's holding a disposable waterproof camera. His aim? To get a few happy snaps of his friends surfing.)

PHOTO BY TOM SERVAIS

TAJ BURROW SAYS: "It's a feeling of
speed, power and light. On the west
coast, when the sun's setting and you're
launching straight into the sunlit gold, it
can feel like you're touching heaven."
Taj Burrow, Western Australia.

PHOTO BY SCOTT AICHNER

RABBIT SAYS: "Occy's thrilled us. He's thrilled us like no other surfer – maybe ever." Mark Occhilupo, perfect form, remote Indonesia.

PHOTO BY ROB KEITH

THE WORD

A FOREWORD BY COMPANY FOUNDER GORDON MERCHANT.

THE MOST AMAZING THING ABOUT THE BILLABONG STORY IS JUST HOW HUMBLE ITS BEGINNINGS WERE. WE WERE LITERALLY JUST CUTTING OUT BOARDSHORTS ON THE KITCHEN TABLE, TRYING TO COBBLE TOGETHER A LIVING THAT ALLOWED MAXIMUM SURF TIME. WE NEVER HAD ANY THOUGHTS OF THE KIND OF COMPANY IT HAS GROWN INTO. ONE OF THE MOST SATISFYING ASPECTS OF THAT GROWTH IS THE NUMBER OF SURFERS AND OTHER PEOPLE BILLABONG NOW PROVIDES A LIVELIHOOD FOR. BILLABONG INTERNATIONAL EMPLOYS OVER 1000 PEOPLE WORLDWIDE, AND INDIRECTLY HELPS SUPPORT MANY MORE - FROM PHOTOGRAPHERS TO FILM MAKERS, SUPPLIERS AND CONTRACTORS.

IT IS PARTICULARLY GRATIFYING THAT MANY PEOPLE WHO HAVE CONTRIBUTED SO MUCH ARE NOW ABLE TO OWN A STAKE IN THE COMPANY AND SHARE IN ITS SUCCESS AND GROWTH. A FRIEND OF MINE TOMMY MOSES WAS THE FIRST SURFER I KNEW WHO MADE CLOTHES, WHEN HE STARTED CREME CLOTHING. I TALKED HIM INTO DOING THAT. HE WAS AN APPRENTICE TAILOR IN SYDNEY AND HE SAVED $300 AND WAS GOING TO THE GOLD COAST FOR A BIT OF A SURFING HOLIDAY. I TALKED HIM INTO STARTING HIS OWN LABEL. IT WASN'T SURF SPECIFIC CLOTHING, WE WERE JUST HAVING FUN MAKING CLOTHES WE LIKED. THERE WAS NO ONE DOING THAT AT THE TIME AND I SAW THE SUCCESS HE STARTED TO HAVE. THAT WAS PART OF THE INSPIRATION FOR GIVING IT A GO MYSELF. NO ONE WAS MAKING CLOTHES FOR SURFERS. IF YOU KNEW SOMEONE IN THE U.S YOU MIGHT BE ABLE TO GET HOLD OF A PAIR OF HANG TEN BOARDSHORTS.

MRS PLATT WAS THE FIRST PERSON IN AUSTRALIA TO START MAKING BOARDSHORTS SPECIFICALLY FOR SURFERS. BY THE TIME WE STARTED BILLABONG, THERE WERE ABOUT A DOZEN LABELS MAKING BOARDSHORTS, BUT NONE OF THEM HAD ANYTHING TO DO WITH SURFING,

AND THEY WERE LOUSY. THEY USED COTTON THREAD THAT ROTTED IN SALTWATER AND THEY NEVER HAD A GOOD FIT. YOU'D FEEL LIKE A DORK WEARING THEM UP AROUND YOUR BELLY BUTTON, AND THEY'D ALWAYS CREEP UP, WHICH WAS VERY UNCOMFORTABLE. THEY WEREN'T DESIGNED TO SURF IN AT ALL. I REMEMBER ONE YEAR AT THE STUBBIES, MARK RICHARDS RIPPED HIS BOARDSHORTS UP THE SIDE - IT WAS THE ONLY WAY YOU COULD GET ANY LEG MOVEMENT IN THEM, I'LL NEVER FORGET THE SIGHT OF M.R UP ON STAGE ACCEPTING HIS TROPHY WITH THESE SHORTS RIPPED UP THE SIDE.

IT TOOK A LOT OF TRIAL AND ERROR BUT WE EVENTUALLY DEVELOPED A STYLE OF BOARDSHORTS THAT WERE REALLY FUNCTIONAL AND DURABLE FOR SURFING. I WAS JUST FIGURING IT ALL OUT, DOING A CRASH COURSE IN PATTERN MAKING AS I WENT, BUT THEY SEEMED TO WORK. MY FIRST WIFE RENA AND I WERE JUST TRYING TO SAVE ENOUGH MONEY TO BUILD A HOUSE, THAT WAS THE ORIGINAL IDEA FOR STARTING THE BUSINESS. WE REACHED A POINT WHERE WE LOOKED AT EACH OTHER AND REALISED, WE COULD ACTUALLY MAKE A PRETTY DECENT LIVING OUT OF THIS. WE FORGOT ABOUT THE HOUSE BECAUSE EVERY CENT WE MADE HAD TO GO BACK INTO THE COMPANY. TO GROW, THE BUSINESS NEEDED THE MONEY FAR MORE THAN ANYTHING ELSE DID.

THE SURF INDUSTRY WAS BASICALLY CREATED OUT OF A FEW BRANDS THAT WERE VERY COMPETITIVE WITH EACH OTHER. THROUGH THAT COMPETITION THEY JUST ABOUT PUSHED EVERYONE ELSE OUT OF THE MARKETPLACE. THE MAINSTREAM MENSWEAR LABELS KNEW HOW TO MAKE CLOTHES BUT THEY DIDN'T KNOW ANYTHING ABOUT FASHION OR MARKETING OR FUNCTIONAL SURFWEAR.

GORDON AND OCC/ BURLEIGH/SCOTT NEEDHAM

BACK THEN, EVERY TOWN HAD AT LEAST ONE OR TWO MENSWEAR SHOPS AS WELL AS JEANERIES OR OTHER CLOTHING STORES. SURFSHOPS, ON THE OTHER HAND, WERE HARD TO COME BY. IF YOU WERE LUCKY YOU'D FIND SOME GUY MAKING SURFBOARDS, USUALLY IN A BUILDING AT THE WRONG END OF TOWN. HE WOULD PUT IN A FEW BOARDIES AND TEES, USUALLY "ON CONSIGNMENT" WITH A COUPLE OF THE SURFBOARDS HE HAD FOR SALE. THE AREA PUT ASIDE FOR THIS USUALLY HAD SEA-GRASS MATTING ON THE FLOOR THAT WAS COVERED WITH A MIXTURE OF SAND AND FOAM DUST WITH THE PUNGENT SMELL OF POLYESTER RESIN WAFTING THROUGH THE AIR. NOW THOSE MENSWEAR OUTLETS ARE VERY FEW AND A LOT OF THE FASHION RETAILING IS DONE THROUGH SURFSHOPS. IT'S REALLY CHANGED THE MARKETPLACE. IN THE EARLY DAYS, NO ONE WANTED TO TAKE YOU SERIOUSLY AS A SURFWEAR MANUFACTURER. I REMEMBER GOING TO THE BANK TO GET A LOAN FOR THE COMPANY AND THEY JUST LAUGHED AT ME. CLOTHING WAS A NASTY WORD FOR THE BANKS, BECAUSE SO MANY CLOTHING MANUFACTURERS WENT BROKE. AND SURFERS WERE EVEN WORSE. THEY HAD NO TIME FOR SURFERS. SO IF YOU WERE A SURF CLOTHING MANUFACTURER, YOU WERE THEIR WORST NIGHTMARE. IT TOOK US QUITE A LONG TIME BEFORE WE FOUND A BANK TO LEND US ANY MONEY. WE CHANGED BANKS FOUR TIMES BEFORE WE FOUND A BANK THAT WOULD HELP US.

ALL THE PEOPLE THAT BILLABONG HAS EMPLOYED OVER THE YEARS HAVE REALLY BEEN THE FOUNDATION OF THE COMPANY'S SUCCESS. WE HAVE BEEN BLESSED TO HAVE A LOT OF REALLY EXCELLENT PEOPLE PUT THEIR ENERGY INTO IT. YOU CAN'T BUILD A COMPANY BY YOURSELF, PEOPLE ARE THE FOUNDATION. YOU TRY TO CREATE A TEAM SITUATION WHERE EVERYONE FEELS PART OF IT, AND I THINK WE'VE MANAGED TO DO THAT. I'M ENORMOUSLY GRATEFUL TO ALL THE RETAILERS AND BILLABONG CUSTOMERS WHO HAVE SUPPORTED US OVER THE YEARS. NONE OF THIS WOULD BE POSSIBLE WITHOUT THEM.

ALSO, ALL OUR INTERNATIONAL LICENSEES ALL OVER THE WORLD HAVE PLAYED A REALLY IMPORTANT PART IN OUR SUCCESS. OUR CURRENT BOARD AND SENIOR MANAGEMENT HAVE DONE A WONDERFUL JOB GUIDING BILLABONG THROUGH THE TRANSITION INTO BEING A PUBLIC COMPANY.

MY EX-WIFE AND COFOUNDER OF BILLABONG, RENA, DESERVES GREAT RECOGNITION FOR HER ROLE TOO. SHE WAS ALWAYS POSITIVE AND A TOWER OF STRENGTH IN A LOT OF SITUATIONS WHEN THINGS WERE LOOKING GRIM. AND I REMAIN INDEBTED TO ALL THE SPONSORED TEAM SURFERS WHO EVER WORE THE BILLABONG LABEL AND REPRESENTED US SO WELL THROUGHOUT THE SURFING WORLD.

BILLABONG HAS SO DOMINATED MY LIFE OVER THE PAST 30 YEARS THERE HAVE BEEN A LOT OF SWELLS MISSED, A LOT OF HARD WORK, LATE NIGHTS, SWEAT AND STRESS. ITS WONDERFUL BEING ABLE TO TAKE A STEP BACK AND SEE HOW FAR WE'VE COME, AND TO HAVE A BIT MORE TIME TO SURF AND RELAX AND ENJOY LIFE, KNOWING THE COMPANY'S FATE IS IN GOOD HANDS. AS I APPROACH 60, I'M ENJOYING MY SURFING MORE THAN EVER.

OBVIOUSLY, THE SURF BUSINESS HAS BEEN VERY GOOD TO ME AND I REMAIN GRATEFUL FOR EVERYTHING SURFING HAS GIVEN ME IN MANY WAYS. I BELIEVE THE ACT OF SURFING ITSELF HAS HELPED FUEL THE AMAZING SUCCESS OF THE SURF INDUSTRY. THE OCEAN HAS AN ENDLESS CAPACITY TO KEEP YOU HONEST, TO KEEP THINGS REAL. FOR ME, GOING FOR A SURF HAS ALWAYS BEEN THE BEST MEANS TO GET PERSPECTIVE ON POTENTIALLY DAUNTING BUSINESS ISSUES. ITS GREAT TO BE ABLE TO EMPTY YOUR HEAD, GET OUT THERE AND STOP THINKING ABOUT BUSINESS. IT JUST SEEMS TO STIR UP THE OXYGEN IN YOUR BLOOD AND YOU SEEM TO HAVE MUCH BETTER THOUGHTS ANYWAY WHEN YOU DO GO BACK TO WORK. YOU HAVE A FRESH PERSPECTIVE. AS OUR INDUSTRY CONTINUES TO GROW, PRESENTING ONCE UNIMAGINED OPPORTUNITIES AND CHALLENGES, NOW MORE THAN EVER, MY KEY ADVICE WOULD BE: KEEP SURFING.

GORDON MERCHANT, ANGOURIE, NSW, AUGUST, 2003

CONTENTS

LAID BY BILLABONG EVENTS, THE TOUR STOPS AT KIRRA, JEFFREYS BAY, MUNDAKA AND TEAHUPO'O.

100 THE SUPER CHALLENGE
BILLABONG WANTED TO TEST A REJUVENATED MARK OCCHILUPO AGAINST THE WORLD'S BEST. WHAT'D THEY DO? CREATE AN INVITATION-ONLY EVENT THAT GREW INTO LEGEND.

110 DOING IT FOR THE KIDS
IF YOU WANT SURFING TO PROGRESS, YOU'VE GOTTA NURTURE THE KIDS. THE BILLABONG JUNIOR SERIES CREATED A FRAMEWORK FOR THE GROWING OF TEENAGERS WITH POTENTIAL. ITS STAR GRADUATES? CURRENT WORLD NUMBERS ONE AND TWO, ANDY IRONS AND JOEL PARKINSON.

116 SURFING AND THE GIRLS: A LOVE STORY
GIRLS ALWAYS SURFED. SUDDENLY, AROUND 1992, IT BECAME A PHENOMENON.

126 THE ODYSSEY
MEN ON JETSKIS, ON STANDBY, READY TO CHASE THE BIGGEST SURF ON THE PLANET. THEIR GOAL? TO RIDE A 100-FOOT WAVE.

136 EAT, SLEEP, SURF AND WATCH SURF VIDEOS
THE PROGRESSION OF SURFING IS CONSTANT AND EGALITARIAN THANKS TO THE MIRACLE OF EASILY-AVAILABLE SURF MOVIES.

THE ⬚ TRIP:

A STORY OF A MAN AND HIS WIFE GORDON + RENA AND THEIR DESIRE TO FUND A **LIFESTYLE** BASED AROUND THE OCEAN......

"ALL LIFE CAME FROM THE OCEAN ALL LIFE RETURNS TO THE OCEAN"

BY TIM BAKER

The teenage star of Billabong's first video
Surf into Summer , Jason Buttonshaw, Duranbah,
Gold Coast, 1985
MTVZ

Gordon Merchant (arms raised and mouth agape) and teamriders.
(from left): Joe Engel, Thornton Fallander, Peter Harris,
Eric Van Druten, Dwayne Harris, 1981
AITIONN

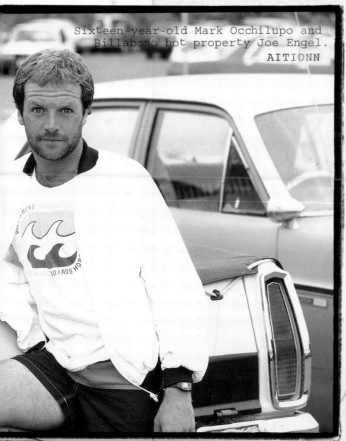

Sixteen-year-old Mark Occhilupo and
Billabong hot property Joe Engel.
AITIONN

Ralph Pullinger, Burleigh cyclone swell, 1987.
AITIONN

1. Wayne McKewen, Spot Klease, Sam Watts
1.1 Occy

2. Billabong ad shoot 2003
Occy, Mick, Andy, Luke, Taj,
Shane, Joel

3. Occy

4. Eric, Ross,
Dwayne,
Joe, Swag

5. Gordon Merchant,
South wall Ballina, AITIONN

7. Luke Egan

10.

THIS SUMMER
IT'S RUBBER

14.

14. Sean "Reg" Riley

18.
Jodie Cooper / Munga/
Jim Banks, Occy

19.
Craig "Scat" Pitchers

20. Matt Branson

Chris "Swag"
Gudenswager

15.

6.
Occy

16. Gary Clisby

Billabong since 1973

8. John Shortis
11. Magoo, Butto
12. Billabong's first
fashion shoot

9. Munga, Magoo, Occy

10. Peter and Dwayne
Harris AITIONN

13. Burleigh boardriders

13.1. Peter King

A 90 minute
2½ years we
the classic mo
Featuring the
Maalaea
and
Uluwatu

Released by Phoenix

BILLABONG

BAD BILLYS

BILLABONG
Surf into Summer

17

17. First Billabong
Pro. Duranbah
1984

22. Occy

JOHNNY CHARLTON
GORDON. DICK VAN STRA
? JOHN STEWART'
MITCH. MATTY LUI

BILLABONG
SINCE 1973
AUSTRALIA

Occys
got a new
steamer

22.

BUD McCRAE, 1ST BB HAWAII REP.
BOB. GORDON BOBS KEN

RAB, JACK. GORDON.
ELIZA

15

19.

20.

25

25. tiffanys motel
Sunny Garcia

26. Early skate shoot

SURFER
HOT

SKELETOR

BAD BILLYS

BAD BILLYS

WHEELER

26.

23.

14th - 18 FEB - A.

21.

21. Randall Kim

23. Joe Engel, Burleigh
SURFINFO.COM.AU

24. Richie Collins

Sunny Garcia

There is a strong case to be made that the success of Billabong was spawned by a magical era of surfing enjoyed by its founder Gordon Merchant. Throughout surfing's history there are a relative handful of Golden Moments – specific times and places where a blessed few surfers sampled the surfing life at its most sublime. Windows in time when a combination of perfect waves, lack of crowds and a free-and-easy lifestyle granted a select few entry into the realm of their most idyllic surfing dreams. California in the '40s or '50s, Hawaii in the '50s and '60s, France in the early '80s, the first forays to remote parts of Indonesia in the '80s and '90s... and Australia's Gold Coast in the early '70s. For those few years, when surfboards first became short and refined enough to ride deep in the tube, but before the crowds descended, the Gold Coast's point-breaks were buffeted by consistent swells during a period of heavy cyclonic activity. The surfers who enjoyed this magical era, including Rabbit Bartholomew, Michael Peterson and Peter Townend, rightly considered themselves among the luckiest souls to ever walk the earth, gorging on perfect, sand-bottom barrels in warm water with no crowds day after sun-drenched day.

16

Gordon Merchant, freshly arrived from Sydney's Maroubra Beach, was in the thick of it, living firstly out of his car then in a rented farmhouse in the lush Gold Coast hinterland, shaping a couple of boards a week in a cow shed to keep himself in food and petrol. "It was amazing. When I got here in 1970 there was only about 15 guys that used to surf Kirra and Burleigh because of the

consequences of losing your boards," Gordon remembers, of the Gold Coast surf scene before legropes. "When the surf was pumping there'd be 200 people, most of them surfers, sitting round the points watching you surf and not going out because they didn't want to smash their boards... I didn't know it at the time but I was entering the best five years of surf in my life and that any surfer had ever seen on the Gold Coast. I was 26, in the prime of my life, capable of surfing nine hours a day, four days straight. I had great boards, a leash and the crowds weren't a factor. I was as free as a bird and, needless to say, loving life."

Gordon was one of the first surfers to master the intricacies of reading the weather maps to forecast surf conditions up and down the coast, giving him the uncanny knack of turning up where and when the waves were pumping. From the Gold Coast points to northern NSW, Gordon became renowned for turning up when the waves turned on. "Gordon was everywhere. He could read the weather maps better than anyone," remembers Rabbit Bartholomew. "He'd be at Angourie, he'd be at Kirra, he'd be at Snapper, he'd be at Burleigh. I realised, this reading the weather maps gives you the edge." Through this period, Gordon was instrumental in the development of the three most essential pieces of surfing equipment: the surfboard, the legrope and the boardshort, ushering in revolutionary changes that endure to this day. "It was during this period of time that I developed a totally different surfboard design from what was currently available. I also developed, I think, first leash that had a

strap around your ankle attached to a rubber shock absorber and then to a fibreglass plug on the deck of your board. The boards I designed were around 50 percent thinner and 50 percent lighter with small boxy rails and a tucked under edge," Gordon explains. "You had this instant speed and this thing accelerated, and yet you could still lay it on a rail and do a full rail turn because it had some rail to work off. That was the start of it, that changed everything. I remember copping a heap of flack from a lot of the then surfboard design gurus because my boards were so different. I also copped a lot of verbal abuse for being the first surfer to use a leash. But on both accounts I used to just laugh at them because my boards worked well and were going faster. With a leash I could sit deeper and catch heaps of waves."

But surfboard shaping was affecting his health, and Gordon figured there had to be an easier way to make a living. He saw his friend Tommy Moses doing well with one of the first surf labels of the day, Creme. Gordon's mother had been a seamstress and he had grown up around the rag trade. When he met his future wife, Rena, together they decided to give the clothing business a go. "Rena was crocheting and making little bikinis and selling them, and we decided we'd keep on with that, and we started making a few boardshorts and we used to take them round on a Friday afternoon and sell them to the local surf shops," recalls Gordon. "I think it cost us two bucks for the fabric and the velcro and the cotton. We didn't even have any labels on them, it was that archaic. I'd cut them out on the kitchen

Billabong fashion shoot at the height of corduroy's supremacy, 1985 (from left): Gary Green, Richard Marsh, Derek Hynd, Occ, Jodie Cooper, Wayne Jaggard, Rabbit, Mitch Thorson.
AITIONN

Former child prodigy, now manager to the new crop of the Gold Coast stars, Sam Watts (with Vicky).
AITIONN

table and Rena would sew them and we'd get about 25 pairs together and take them round to Hohnesee's or Goodtimes or whoever and we'd just sell them for four bucks each and they'd retail for $6.50. I think we made about a buck a pair or something, but we had enough to live so we survived."

The concept of a brand name and a logo was almost an afterthought. "After a while, people started having a go at me because there were no labels. I looked like a backyarder," says Gordon. "I needed to get a label that looked pretty established. I thought of the brand like you used to have on farms above the gate – I'll try to do something like that." A kid at the local board factory, Cabbage, came up with the name. "It was just a bit of Australiana and I drew it up and put underneath it, 'Since 1973,' because I thought that's what all these established brands have got. I've walked into Neilsen brothers and I've got my shorts there... and I remember them saying, 'What are you doing? It is 1973.' (Laughs) Everybody's got to start somewhere. It was obviously a bit tongue in cheek but it worked."

Gordon applied his analytical mind to making the most durable boardshorts possible, developing his own triple-stitching technique. The hard-wearing shorts were an immediate hit with surfers. "He was so driven and committed into being on the best surf, he put all that energy and commitment into Billabong," says Rabbit. "They decided, let's make a boardshort that can withstand a surfer's punishment. I well remember you used to get a pair of boardshorts for

Christmas and by March you were wearing them like a dress because the crotch would rot out in them, until they came along. Then it was like, wow, man, you can live in these things for a year or maybe two. It was unheard of." Billabong's simple yet powerful marketing, sponsoring great surfers, running ads with great surf shots with a small logo, struck a strong chord with surfers. "I just tried to look at everything from a surfer's perspective rather than anybody else's perspective," says Gordon. "I tried to think about what appealed to you when you were a grommet, when you just started to surf."

At the same time, Gordon was having to get his head around every aspect of the fast-growing business. "I just did whatever was required, pretty much. I was the sewing machine mechanic, I was the pattern maker, I was the stock room, I did the despatch, and all in a pair of boardshorts. We had this factory and buyers would come in and want to buy product and they'd look straight at me and go, 'Where's the manager?' So I'd look at the girls and go, 'Who wants to be the be the manager today?' and they'd all put their hands up. They'd just look straight past you and look for the guy in the suit."

It's been a heady ride in the 30 years since those humble beginnings – international expansion, exponential growth, the spectacularly successful stock market float as a public company. Ask Gordon for his proudest moments and his pure surf ethic comes through. "I thought that some of the contests in Hawaii were about

as challenging as you'd ever want a contest to be," he says. "If you've got a contest that can be at Sunset, Pipe or Waimea and you are taking boards for all those breaks and you've got to be able to surf all those breaks, that's a big ask. And to watch perfect Waimea at 25 feet and that day that we had to call it on (in 1986), it was hairy."

Any surfer will tell you, when you take off on a big wave, or pull into a gaping barrel, holding your line is key. It's a lesson that's served Gordon well in business too. "Every day, for me personally, I just try to stay as fit as I possibly can, and get the best surf I can," he says. "I'm really happy that I'm still surfing. I don't know how far I can go. When I was a kid, 16, 17, I used to think you stopped surfing at 30, and here I am heading towards 60 and still riding shortboards and enjoying it, going to G-land and places like that. And I don't know how long I can go for but I'll go for as long as I possibly can."

Though Gordon is less hands-on these days, dividing his time between his favourite surf retreats in northern NSW, the Gold Coast and Hawaii, his instincts remain as sharp as ever. "There's a lot to be said for understanding your customer," says the man whose market research is his bliss.

Ronnie Burns, Bunyip Dreaming, photo/movie shoot, north-west Wa. SURFINFO.COM.AU

Marcus Brabant, Rabbit, Munga, Luke. JOLI

Butto and Bad Billys. AITIONN

Luke and Rabbit / South Australia. JOLI

Occy, 16 photographed at Summercloud Bay, NSW, 1983. AITIONN

STAY "HUMAN"

TWENTY MEN AND WOMEN WHO'VE SHAPED THE ART OF BOARDRIDING

ON WATER, SNOW AND CONCRETE

mark occhilupo

"I WAS 15. I'D JUST BEEN KNOCKED OUT OF AN AMATEUR EVENT AND I WAS OVER IT. MY MANAGER RANG GORDON AND SAID THAT I WANTED TO GO ON TOUR. GORDON WENT WITH HIS HEART AND, 21 YEARS LATER, I'M THE THIRD LONGEST-STANDING EMPLOYEE. BEEN ON THE TEAM LONGEST AND STILL PART OF THE WORLD'S BEST SURF TEAM. I'M PRIVILEGED TO BE MIXING IT WITH THE YOUNG GUYS. THEY RIP, THEY'RE WAY MORE TALENTED THAN I AM AND I JUST LOVE SEEING ANDY RIDE TEAHUPO'O AND PIPELINE. OR WHAT TAJ AND PARKO DO IN THE AIR. IT RUBS OFF ON YOU. AND EVEN THOUGH I'M OLDER, I DO LOOK UP TO THEM. A PEER SHOULD BE ABLE TO GIVE CREDIT WHERE CREDIT'S DUE. AND I CAN'T DO IT ENOUGH..."

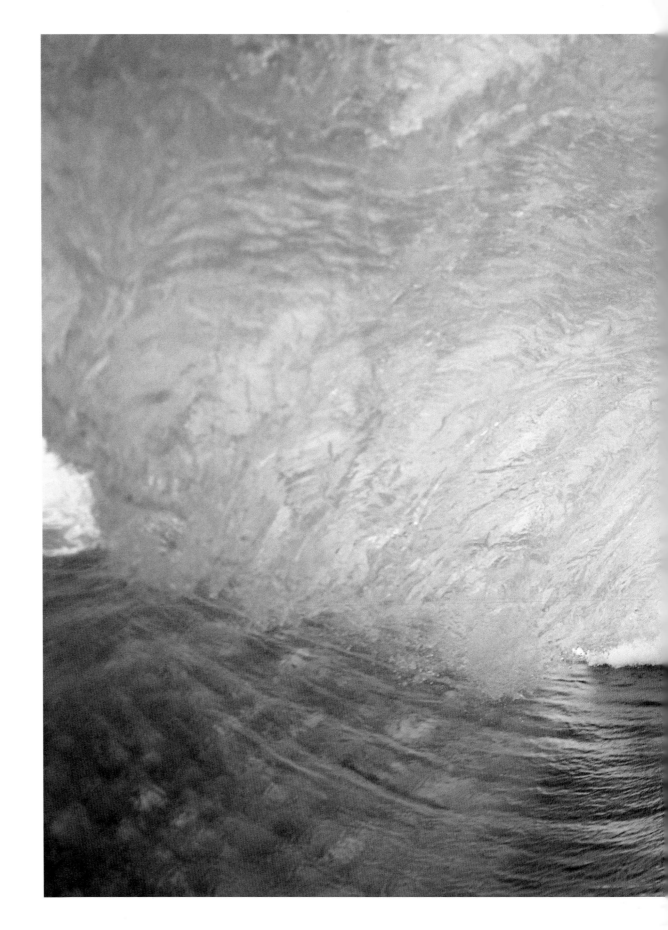

Mark Occhilupo, sport's greatest comeback; an inspiration for three generations of surfers; a world champion at 33. Here Occ gets as deep as man possibly can at the world's most dangerous reef, Passe Hava'e aka Teahupo'o, Tahiti.

DAREN CRAWFORD

Mark Occhilupo, wins at Teahupo'o (and later claims wins in Fiji and Mundaka) en route to his 1999 world title.

TIM MCKENNA

22 **In July 2003, during a break in the Billabong Pro J-Bay, 37-year-old Marco Jay Luciano Occhilupo walked down to the water's edge at Jeffreys Bay, South Africa, a small figure held carefully in his muscular arms.** Just another proud dad and his child? Sure. Yet here in some ways was the closing chapter of a long, extraordinary tale.

Born and raised in Kurnell, living now on the Gold Coast with partner Mae and baby son Jay, Occy's the senior member of the current WCT tribe – the oldest successful WCT competitor in history, in fact. He has a world championship, the respect of all his peers, and a backlog of competitive experience unrivalled by any pro surfer before or since – not to mention, still, the best backside re-entry in the business.

In the process, he's somehow managed to achieve something few surfers have ever had to face: reconciled the needs of the real world with a talent so outsize it's seemed at times to threaten not just his opponents, but himself. Occy learned to surf at nine years of age with the help of big sister Fleur, who pushed him onto the small waves of Kurnell, a tiny suburb on the southern fringe of Botany Bay. He graduated to nearby Cronulla Beach, and began riding stumpy little twin-fins made by local surfer-shaper Jim Banks. By 1982 he was beginning to frighten surfers almost twice his age in Australian pro-am events, and the following year he qualified for the big-time pro event, the Coke Classic at Narrabeen, where he came within a hair of smashing top name Shaun Tomson. Occ was swiftly nicknamed "Rocky" and "the Raging Bull" by the hyperbole-loving Aussie press, and he was off.

In 1984, as a cocky 17-year-old, Occy shot to the top of the ASP ratings. He set performance standards over the next two years that still haven't been matched. At Jeffreys Bay, his power and aggression turned backhand surfing into an advantage. In Hawaii, he won the Pipe Masters on his second trip to the North Shore. Even in America, where Tom Curren had run down a similar track, Occy was adored. In surfing's biggest spectator event, the Op Pro at Huntington Beach, the two engaged in a rivalry of brilliant dimensions. Brilliant, and profitable: professional surfing was peaking, and Curren and Occy were superheroes, delivering the surf industry a promotional platform for unprecedented wealth. Then, in 1988, it was over. Occy's light flamed out as quickly as it'd been lit. The world title that'd seemed the natural reward for his talent had passed him by. Sick of the tour, he threw a quarterfinal heat at the Op and headed back home to Cronulla.

Over the next few years, Occ moved away to the Gold Coast, made a couple of half-hearted comeback attempts, and remained in the public eye as a repeating star of Jack McCoy's Billabong videos. His abilities were clearly still intact as he was featured demolishing Reunion Island, Grajagan, J-Bay and other secret locations around the world.

But this newly invented free-surfing Occy would soon fade. By 1993, the once-driven surfing genius was lying on the couch, watching TV and barely feeling the surfing urge. He stayed there for more than a year before beginning a training regime under McCoy in West Oz, encouraged by his then-wife Beatrice. From his 115-kilo peak, Occ shed 30 kilos and regained his form, and in the process, his spirit.

But how to test the waters? The 1995 Billabong Challenge, held in perfect large West Oz desert lefts, was crafted by Gordon Merchant at least partly to give Occy a sense of the opposition he'd face in a world tour comeback. Against the likes of Kelly Slater, Rob Machado and Sunny Garcia, he responded superbly. Occ went on to qualify for the WCT in 1996, capping it off with a second place at Pipe after coming through the trials.

In 1997, Occy was runner-up to Kelly Slater for the world title, the highlight of his season being a $US55,000 payday in a specialty Skins event at Bells Beach. The next year, he earned his first world tour victory in a dozen years by winning the Rip Curl Pro, also at Bells, and dedicating the win to his stern father Luciano, who he'd long felt disapproved of his pro surfing career. In 1999 Occy followed up to claim victories in Tahiti, Fiji and Mundaka and collect the world crown he'd once been denied. A hero was home. **– Nick Carroll.**

The fluoro green boardshorts, the remarkable torso and a surfboard drawn into a familiar jagged line – as perfect a surfer in 2003 as he was in '84 when he began demolishing a generation of Great Surfers.

JASON MURRAY

layne beachley

Layne brings with her all the history and hopes of every powerful woman that has ever existed on earth. Plenty can achieve trophies but only a select few achieve royalty. A Queen to Kelly's King and all Aussie pride, Layne is spearheading the new woman's movement in surfing. The movement that is altering the entire industry and altering the way every one of us look at women in the line-up.

Consider the fact that Layne is a woman who stands only 5'4", and consider the fact that she's regularly towing-in to 20-foot waves and consider the fact that she is the only woman on earth searching for the 100-foot wave with the rest of the Billabong Odyssey crew – the only one!

Consider all that and just try to deny that that makes her the most courageous surfer on the planet. With legions of new followers, Layne holds the Holy Grail: the world title (five, in fact) and that which all women pray for… respect across the board.

A smart cookie, she hasn't frittered away her time and money either. With five houses peppering the northern beaches of Sydney and the Queensland coast, she surveys her realm from the balcony of her own three-level mansion in Curl Curl. And when it all becomes too much she flies up to her jungle retreat on a little known island just off Queensland, one of the grooviest surf pads in the world with a perfect point right out front.

A sufferer of Chronic Fatigue syndrome, it hasn't been easy. Yet pound for pound, Layne is one of the physically strongest female athletes in the world. Just ask the Queen of England, who has publicly and privately recognised Layne's achievements in the fields of female endeavour.

Unlike other heroes who have come and gone, to a sporting nation like Australia, Layne is more than a woman, she is a symbol. A tattoo. The personification of the only three things that will ever make an athlete great, that will ever make a country great: Strength, Wisdom and Pride. **– Matt George.**

Five-time world champion Layne Beachley, the only woman on the planet to put herself into waves like this: towing-in at an outer reef, Hawaii.
(ACTION) ART BREWER (PORTRAIT) SCOTT NEEDHAM/SNP5000.COM

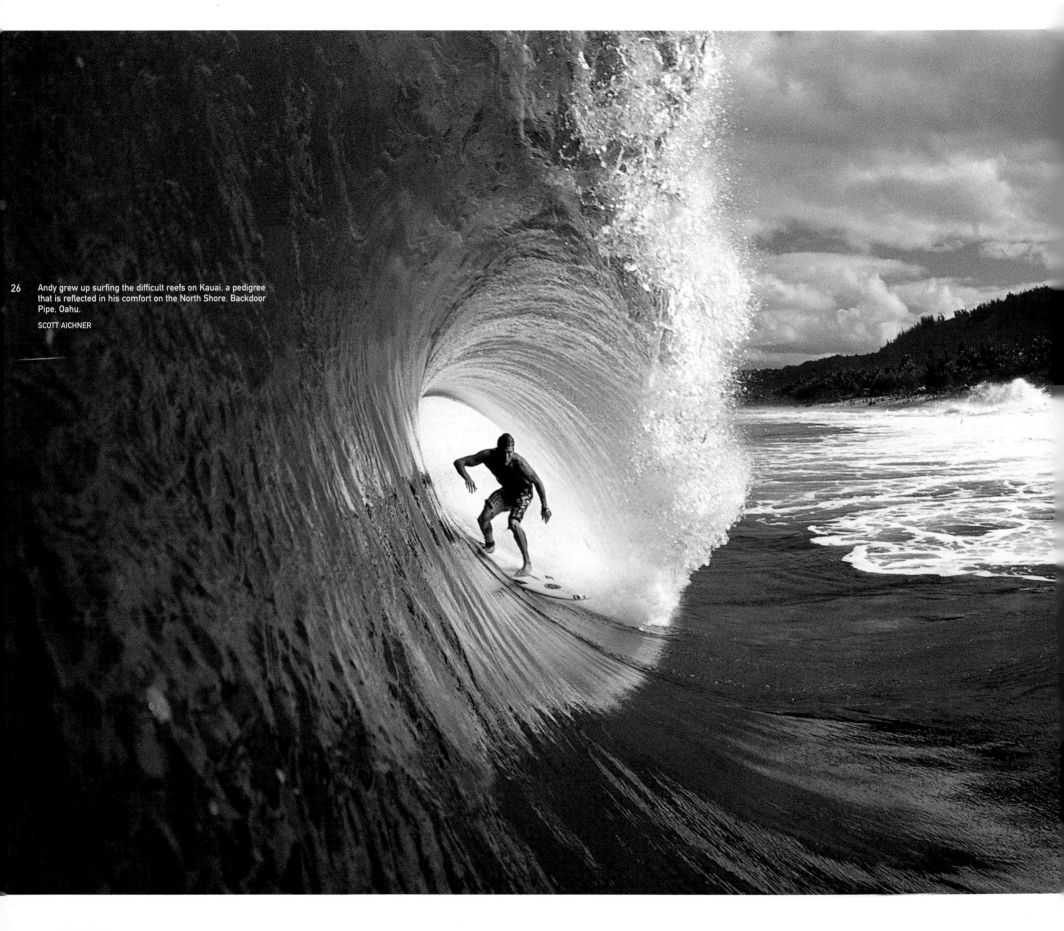

26   Andy grew up surfing the difficult reefs on Kauai, a pedigree
that is reflected in his comfort on the North Shore. Backdoor
Pipe, Oahu.

SCOTT AICHNER

andy irons

Why does Andy wear the world crown so lightly? Maybe because if there's one surfer in the world who represents all of what the surfing world expects from a young world champ in 2003, he's it.

At 25 years of age, Andy Irons has done the full tour of duty, rolling through teen success, early superstardom, a time of uncertainty, and an unstoppable comeback. Despite hundreds of hours in ASP WCT contest jerseys and thousands more in airport transit lounges around the globe, his surfing and attitude both look fresh as a grom's.

AI grew up surfing the warm-water playground of Pinetrees, inside Hanalei on Kauai's north shore, with younger brother Bruce. The quick-reflex little left and right peelers – plus the sibling rivalry – helped develop a surfing approach of incredible range. Andy produces combinations like nobody else right now, rarely doing the same turn twice in a row, constantly adapting his ultra-flexible style to any wave, anywhere. "Before, in my earlier years, I used to try to put a wave together, you know?" he explains. "I'd put a ride together the way I thought the judges wanted to see it, a certain turn here, another turn there. It would work but always felt like I was trying too hard. Now I'm just reacting to the wave spontaneously – sensing the speed of the wave and matching it with the turn speed. Not trying to think too much about it, though. That seems the key. (But) there's always room for improvement. Whenever I watch videos I see the little mistakes… there's never a point in surfing when you can't work on something." Added to that skill range is a killer confidence, something Andy freely admits hasn't always been present. After explosive early success – winning the Op Pro, US Open and the Billabong World Juniors in 1998, his first real tour year – he found himself sucked into the party tour. Soon he was losing to surfers out of what seemed like nothing more than bad karma. At the end of '99, his rating dropped out of the WCT top 44, and for a humiliating year Andy had to work his way back up through the qualifying series. Humiliating, but helpful. "You gotta have fun," he says today. "Otherwise it's not fulfilling... But you've also got to learn to have a couple of beers rather than a case."

Things began turning around for him in late 2000, with a telling, dramatic round-four win over Kelly Slater at Pipeline. Soon afterward he signed on with Billabong, a step that seemed not just in synch with any young pro's need for career security, but with Andy's particular need for a home base, a fresh start. Suddenly he was part of a team that included guys like Taj Burrow and Joel Parkinson – surfers of his age, his creativity, his energy level. It was the step Andy needed in order to fire up both his surfing and his great, dormant psychological strength: a relentless, positive willingness to succeed. **– Nick Carroll.**

shane dorian

Shane Dorian, with his easy smile, his loyalty to his friends, his loose style and his unquestioned courage in hairy waves, has captured the imagination of the surfing world. And in doing so, he has gained that rare respect among his peers that transcends mere competitive feats. To see him push over the ledge at Waimea, or haul into gaping maws at Pipe or Teahupo'o or Kandui's is to see the kind of commitment, the kind of spirit, the kind of surfing that takes one's breath away.

Often reserved and introspective, Shane plays his cards close to his chest. He can afford to. He knows he has a winning hand. Hungry for speed, Shane's surfing is in a constant state of acceleration from take-off to kick-out as he finds impossible power points in impossible waves from two feet to 60. A skill honed switchblade-sharp that has earned him gold at two of the most prestigious contests on earth: Bells Beach and the Billabong Challenge. Spiritually adventurous, he once dropped off the tour to play the lead character in In God's Hands, a Columbia Tri-star feature release. By insisting that he would perform all his own stunts, he brought an honesty to the film that singlehandedly saved it from being just another silly Hollywood exercise. Honesty. Maybe that is what being from the Big Island of Hawaii is all about. As isolated as it is, and not well known for world-class surf spots, Shane rose from the shade of the Hau tree at his beloved Banyans to the very heights of the professional surfing scene; carrying within him the Mana of an island of fire. A place he calls home. A place he is forever faithful to. Perhaps this fire is what lives in his heart, fuels his dreams, drives his passion for excellence.

As easy going as he may seem, with his rock star looks and quiet confidence, his dedication to his physical well-being borders on the obsessive. Like a middleweight boxer, Shane always shows up ready to rumble, whipcord-lean, strength tuned, mind focused. His significance in the surfing world, indeed what might become his legacy in the years ahead, is not only his surfing, but the way he has lived his life as a man. Trustworthy, solid as a rock both spiritually and physically, and loyal above all. As Shane continues to ride waves with a wild elegance, as his legend grows, as his ongoing competitive achievements swell, the world will watch on, unable to look away every time he paddles out. Because Shane carries with him more than just surfing skills. Shane carries the example of a life that is being well lived. **– Matt George.**

Drive, composure and light-footed acceleration through a symmetrically-perfect Indonesian barrel. Hawaiian Shane Dorian, technically-sharp and well-schooled in the physics of dangerous waves.

(ACTION) JASON CHILDS (PORTRAIT) STEVE SHERMAN

ronnie burns

Surfing aside, Ronnie Burns caught the public's attention just once, in the summer of 1990, after he pinballed his trailbike down a rocky hillside behind Kawela Bay, crashed, and died a few hours later from hypothermia. The lanky 27-year-old goofy-footer was eulogised in the surf press as fun-loving and cheerful, but also private and somewhat removed. Burns did his thing, the rest of the surf world did its thing, and there was overlap, but not that much. He didn't get a posthumous invite to the Quiksilver/Eddie Aikau event, like Mark Foo did. (Burns competed in the 1990 Aikau just a few months before he died, and finished eighth – Foo got 14th.) Trendsetting Hawaiian surfers didn't get commemorative tattoos when Burns died, the way Todd Chesser's buddies did a few years later. "Ronnie Burns doesn't have an image problem," I wrote in a 1987 Surfer magazine profile, after shocking readers by revealing Burns' bizarre penchant for Mexican food, pick-up basketball, The Flintstones, and the colour blue, "because Ronnie Burns doesn't have an image."

What he *did* have was a unassailable North Shore reputation, from Sunset Beach to Rocky Point to Waimea, with full demigod status at Pipeline. Never mind that Burns was a pro tour washout and didn't have an act in the bubbly sandbar peaks of Sydney or Huntington. Along the plumeria-scented shores of the North Shore, and among those who knew, Burns was known as an unassuming but all-in master.

First-born son to Boscoe Burns, ace laminator for Hobie Surfboards, six-year-old Ronnie began to surf in 1969, not long after moving with his family from Orange County to the North Shore. Boscoe promised Ronnie a round-trip ticket to anywhere in the world if he finished high school, and graduation day found the teenager lodged in Bali's Kuta Beach, on his way to Uluwatu ("The deal was I had to graduate," Burns later explained. "Nobody said anything about going to the ceremony.") By the mid-'80s he was part of a ruling Pipeline

triumvirate that included Tom Carroll and Derek Ho. Burns was the patient one who sat a few yards outside the pack and let medium-sized sets roll by, waiting for the biggest, cleanest wave. Carroll and Ho were both quicker and flashier then Burns, and more likely to nuke the beach gallery with some kind of unholy blow-hole miracle barrel. The slightly bow-legged Burns – eight inches taller than Carroll and a full 10 inches taller than Ho – rode with a greater measure and deliberation, often using a chunky mid-face stall while dropping in, so that even his longest and deepest pits looked more inevitable than miraculous. Still, nobody in the '80s had a better deep-tube success rate than Burns, and that kept him in the first rank at Pipeline for most of his young life.

Burns is remembered almost exclusively as a North Shore surfer, but I've always thought his finest moment came during an '87 trip to Grajagan, the highlights of which are featured in a Billabong promo vid titled Filthy Habits. G-land is six-to-eight feet, blue and sparkling, and nobody else appears to be in the water. One ride in particular stands out. Burns leisurely puts together a series of banked turns as he rides through the long Moneytrees section, then drops into the trough where he carves an exquisite below-sea-level arc as the wave squares up to Speed Reef. He lightly comes off the inside rail, takes aim, bends his knees slightly, vanishes while the tube funnels and explodes for 50 yards, then slouches back out into daylight.

Burns' Filthy Habits sequence is playing on my TV right now. Just in front of the TV screen is his Surfer profile, open to the page where we find out how much he enjoys a cold Heineken, and that he actually fixes his own dings. My eyes flick back and forth between the TV screen and the magazine, and I wonder: for some very brief period of time – maybe just those compressed few moments at Speed Reef – was Ronnie Burns simultaneously the blandest and coolest surfer in the world? **– Matt Warshaw.**

"That was a very special day at Pipeline," recalls photographer Don King, of his seminal watershot of Ronnie Burns (far left). "I don't remember the year – late '80s or 1990. It was during the HIC pipe contest in March. Most of the surfers were intimidated by the power of the waves. Many waves went unridden because they were so thick. Ronnie was in his prime. It was magical to watch. He had a special relationship with Pipeline. You can see that in this picture. He's taken off behind the peak, and he's completely in control of his speed and position as he bottom turns to set up for a really deep tube. Look how relaxed he is. Totally at home. Ronnie had a knack for taking off on the heaviest waves and making it look so easy because he was always relaxed and in control. Ronnie went on to win the final against Derek Ho, Brock Little, and Tony Moniz. Ronnie was my favourite surfer to photograph. I think he surfed Pipe as well as anyone ever has." Ronnie Burns, a young life lived well at The Pipe.

ALL PHOTOS DON KING

david rastovich

While the WCT can be a great vehicle for stretching your surfing and accessing the competitive beast within, it can also be growth stunting. Sure you get to travel the world, but you do so in a box – myopically focused on heats and ratings points and all manner of ASP high drama. Duke Kahanamoku's image of the complete Waterman goes straight out the window. Surfing becomes a linear deal, the quest to beat opponents the be all and end all.

Dave Rastovich is a Waterman, and though he's a WCT-calibre surfer, he has no interest in chasing world titles. Instead, he focuses on surfing as a holistic process, a launch pad into the inner depths of the soul. The fact that his father is a healer may have something to do with this. Rasta was raised with a "smell the roses" sensibility. By no means is he the testosterone-riddled, knock-'em-back-at-the-RSL sort. Instead of skull and crossbones he has "Without love we perish" tattooed across his foot. Instead of slapping high fives with his mates he meditates in solitude.

A few facts about Rasta: He was born in New Zealand but spent his formative years riding Gold Coast pointbreaks. He has won contests – quite a few actually – but somewhere along the line he realised there was a bigger picture. "Not into rules and regulations," he says.

Dave got into yoga, meditation and his mind opened wide. He experimented with single fins. Under the tutelage of long-time Burleigh Heads shaper Dick Van Straalen, he used retro-boards as a thread into the history of the sport. He learned to love the trim line. He's a physical monster – all pure stuff, clean foods, no dope. He and Brenden Margieson were among the first to ride filthy, nasty, well-documented waves at Shipstern Bluff in Tasmania. He's not afraid to tow in. In fact he and tow-partner Luke Egan are gearing up to pursue The Billabong Odyssey – ride a 100-foot wave, earn $US500,000.

Rasta's trip is a rare one. His paycheques don't hinge on the tangible, like contest results or photos in the mags. He does what he does, and the attention follows naturally. The fact that he's a surf star is neither the journey nor the destination. It's a by-product of being in tune with himself, and consequently in tune with the ocean.
– Jamie Brisick.

Rasta and a blue-water floater on a remote stretch of coastline off northern Sumatra. "A perfect analogy for The Feeling is when a musician is playing at their best. They're completely lost in the music, lost in the free expression," says Rasta. "They don't have a conscious frame of mind and, instead, behave instinctually, letting the intelligence of the body take over – a kind of surrendering to the creative intelligence that's inside us all. During peak surfing moments, for me, there's an experience of no mind, no thought, just surrendering."

(ACTION) ART BREWER (PORTRAIT) SCOTT NEEDHAM/SNP5000.COM

34 Rabbit – portrait shoot with Surfing World at the height of his competitive powers, world champion year, 1978. And (action) flying the flag for his home state at the wave he calls home, Kirra Point.

(ACTION) JOLI (PORTRAIT) AITIONN

wayne "rabbit" bartholomew

TEAM RIDER – 1985-'93
SPECIAL PROJECTS – 1993-'99

Rabbit has always been a connoisseur of the peak moment, and his time at Billabong delivered many: overlooking Jeffreys Bay as a new swell greeted another Billabong Pro, and hundreds of dolphins surfed their way down the famous point, with lines stacked to the horizon. Gambling everything on the unlikely odds of scoring waves for a Kirra event and being blessed with perfect conditions at the fickle pointbreak, not once, but four years in a row. Standing out in the wind and rain at North Stradbroke Island pleading with the raging night elements to swing the wind offshore, after they had left Burleigh Heads in the face of a howling nor-easter, and awakening to clean, sunny, offshore Point Lookout.

Rabbit's old mate Gordon Merchant picked him up as a team rider as Rabbit struggled to find a career direction after the heady highs of eight straight years in the top five, and a world title in 1978. "Through the difficult times of facing retirement, that old walking the plank bit, Gordon left it open to me to carve a niche out for myself," says Rabbit. "I liked the idea of freewheeling it. I didn't want to move into an office, I wanted to freewheel it and create something."

Rabbit repaid Gordon's faith with a creative, open-ended, alchemical role as special projects co-ordinator, overseeing the pioneering Billabong Challenge events at Jeffreys Bay and WA's northern desert, the innovative Billabong Junior Series, and the landmark Billabong Pro events at Kirra Point and Jeffreys Bay. And Rabbit's collaborations with moviemaker Jack McCoy have left a rich cinematic legacy and helped set the co-ordinates for pro surfing's shift to quality wave locations. "It was a good run, it was a fun time. I was a bit of a jack of all trades," says Rabbit. "The first time I wore Billabong was at the Kirra Teams Challenge. It was perfect Kirra, and in my heat for Snapper I got a perfect 10. That was a pretty nice way to start, a nice omen." Rabbit fell into his contest directing role when he staged his first humble Billabong Kirra Pro with $5000 prizemoney, co-sponsored by the old Hill Street nightclub. "It was really the most epic day. Everyone was getting unbelievable barrels at Kirra," says Rabbit. "It was really nice to see people going, this is the best surfing day of their life and it was during an event. It was in those years where we experimented with not clearing the water and everyone was really cool about it."

In his current executive role as President of the Association of Surfing Professionals (ASP), Rabbit looks back on his Billabong days with no small measure of fondness. Whether it was herding a bunch of grommets to Hawaii for the first time, camping out in the desert with a group of the world's best surfers, or scheduling an expression session at perfect Jeffreys Bay, just so he could sneak in one uncrowded surf down the point, Rab's driving force was always maximum surf time.

Favourite memory? "Out in the desert with The Billabong Challenge crew, hanging out in the desert camp with Jack McCoy and George Simpson, having epic times. We used to call it the Hilton in the desert – beautiful food, surfing, fishing, playing ping pong, having a lot of fun." **– Tim Baker.**

36 Margo uncoils into The Cove's arms, Burleigh Heads, Gold Coast.
ANDREW SHIELD

brenden margieson

There are certain attributes common to most male pro surfers: a hefty ego, the ability to win surf contests and a rat-morality that drives many. But not Brenden "Margo" Margieson. The strapping naturalfooter has always been absurdly modest and self-deprecating, while there are journalists with better competitive records (apart from Margo's memorable blitzkrieg to win the '96 Nias 'QS event at epic, turd-brown Lagundi). And not only does Margo have morals, he even lives by them! He's super-proud of his family (wife Simone, near three-year-old Micah, and a mystery bub brewing in Simone's womb). So how did this weird anti-pro become the most photographed Aussie surfer of the last decade and star of countless surf vids from Jack McCoy's Sons of Fun to Justin Gane's recent Margography, Wanderjahr?

The only thing Margo has ever had going for him is his brilliant freesurfing ability. Thank Huey Billabong recognised this when Margo was still just a teenager. In and around the odd doomed foray on the WQS, Margo has been the Oz Billabong soul surf-tripping flagship for a dozen odd years. It's a role common today with all surf companies, yet Margo was the pioneer who showed the real value of putting a real surfer in real waves. No matter where he's been sent (pretty much everywhere), Margo is guaranteed to rip with his unique mixture of classic power and stylish finesse that have always made him a photographer's wet dream incarnate.

"Thank God mum and dad moved to Byron when I was five," smiles Margo, who was born July 3, 1972 at... Penrith, an outer suburb of Sydney two hours from the beach. After 15 years honing his skills on the North Coast's point breaks, Margo moved further north to the Goldie... to hone 'em even more. Been there ever since. Yet he's such a jovial, sharing cruiser, it's hard to imagine how he ever caught the waves to become so bloody good.

Still, the man with the girl's nickname is no blouse. In the aftermath of the original Tavarua tuberiding contest thingie, the crew got on the kava, beer and anything alcoholic not buried in a vault beneath the sand. Australia had just won a rowing gold at the Olympics, which seemed as good an excuse as any for a patriotic brain-cell sacrifice. Sometime late in the evening, photographer Ted Grambeau collapsed face-first. An enraged Margo, believing a certain obnoxious high-profile American must have king-hit Ted, chased the offender, and wrestled him on the beach, until he was finally convinced that Ted's collapse was a natural, and in fact quite regular, phenomenon. What a mate.

In 2004, Margo will become the co-ordinator of the Billabong Odyssey in Oz, a job that should keep him both on the road and in the water. Margo: "I wanna keep it as low-key and respectful as possible, but it's gonna be more responsibility than I thought. It's not so easy organising a bunch of pro surfers!" Unless, of course, their name is Margo. **– DC Green.**

luke egan

Burleigh Heads, 1986. The Stubbies Pro is in full flight – three-to-five foot and playful, a bulging Gold Coast crowd stretching from The Cove to the pool. In front view, a serious bout between Tom Curren and Barton Lynch. At side view, stage left, a knee-to-waist-high reform being obliterated wave after wave after wave by a loose goofyfooter who seems to be commanding as much attention as the world title chasers. There are laybacks. There are back legs extended into lipslides. There is Luke. Over the course of the next hour-and-a-half, Luke Egan tears the shit out of nothing. He makes diamonds out of dribble, mountains out of miniscule crap. And when Luke finally exits the water, he appears a lot bigger than the size of a man you expect to see doing what he'd just done. You see, the general consensus at the time was that big folks were at a distinct disadvantage in small waves. This is why Simon Anderson invented the thruster – to even the paying field with the 5'8"-and-under set.

Five foot eleven, generously-built Luke Egan did much to destroy this way of thinking. Despite his size, Luke did the newest of new school moves long before New School ever became a term. His surfing in the waist-high-and-under category was revolutionary. And to round out the whole package, he made the finals of the Billabong Pro at Pipe at the tender age of 18, so there was no argument about his big-wave capabilities.

Cut to the present: 33-year-old Luke Egan's a monster. His lust for surfing and competition now spans over two decades and there are no signs of slowing down. His victory in '97 at epic G-Land was hall of fame. His combination of power and innovation has earned him more respect than most world champs. The fact that he's never won one is beside the point. There's an unofficial tally of superbly heroic surfers and on that level Luke's legend. The '86 Burleigh Heads story is relevant in that it was a sign of things to come. While a world title was on the line-up the beach, an exciting show of experimentation and progression was happening down the beach, and though the spectators had come to watch the men in singlets, they were swayed by a spectacular freesurfer, competing against no one but himself.

Surf history abstracts itself. Rather than being about a series of details – who won which event when, for example – it becomes more a montage of great moves, beautiful style… a string of signatures carved across waves. While some names from the '80s, '90s and early 2000s will be written in pencil, and eventually fade, Luke Egan's will be written in fat black texta. And not even time can mess with that. **– Jamie Brisick.**

While the popularity of jetskis has redefined man's approach to big waves, the ski's place in small-wave surfing has been just as crucial. Luke, owner of a 1200cc WaveRunner, is used to turning at high speed. So, when he rides those freak waves with a wedge or sling-shot section and reaches similar speeds to those on a ski, he's one of the few people on this planet who can draw a solid line. Luke Egan, ski-less high-speed gouge, Forster, NSW.

(ACTION) BOSKO (PORTRAIT) SCOTT NEEDHAM/SNP5000.COM

39

keala kennelly

Having been practically raised by Andy and Bruce Irons, it is no wonder Keala is the most electrifying performer in women's surfing today. Famed for her tuberiding ability and possessing a fearlessness in the ocean that borders on the suicidal, Keala embodies what a woman's spirit is capable of in the ocean today. It's not just that she "surfs like a guy". She doesn't. She surfs like a woman possessed. To witness her win at Teahupo'o time and again, to see her drop into tubes at Pipeline, to see her rising to the surface after horrific wipeouts, only to lunge back into the line-up looking for a bigger wave, is to witness a courage beyond the realm of men. The guts it takes to surf side by side with the guys alone is formidable. But to do it, and to surf better than many of those guys, is spectacular.

From her humble beginnings on the island of Kauai, Keala has always burned with a very special fire of life. Growing up in the shadows of the Irons brothers, who still consider her their sister, Keala fought battles on many fronts in order to keep her dream alive. Family strife, giant waves, ethnic bashings, cruel personal effronteries, even a hurricane could not stop her from becoming exactly what she wanted to be.

With a style that is reminiscent of the Ala Moana stars of the '70s, her goofyfooted attack, especially in big hollow lefts, mixes the grace of a woman with the technique of a wild animal. She paddles confidently, smoothes straight down the face, coiled and ready, she squares off her bottom turn, drags her left hand and rides low in the tube. Not choosing the safest lines, but certainly the most dramatic. "If you're not getting crushed now and then, then you aren't trying hard enough," she says. Keala should already be given a lifetime achievement award just for the punishing wipeouts she has suffered. Watching her push the limits, break boundaries and go where no woman has gone before, one is reminded of Mike Purpus's famous quote: "The only way to get out of a radical position is to put yourself there in the first place".

Her approach to competition is unique. "I surf against myself." Regardless, she is the only woman out there whose skills match those of Layne the great, and whether or not Keala surfs alone in her head, their competitive tangles have become legend. Certainly her own woman, Keala has had the courage to live her life on her own terms.

A well-known DJ in ports around the world, Keala has her own life away from competitive surfing that is as electrifying as her surfing itself. Says Keala: "I suppose there is more to life than just surfing waves... but not much." **– Matt George.**

Punk style, in and out of the water. Downtime in Tahiti (left) and gung-ho in the dangerous reef waves of Sumatra, Indonesia.

(ACTION) JOHN BILDERBACK (PORTRAIT) SCOTT NEEDHAM/SNP5000.COM

42   Joel Parkinson, pure lines with a distinctive kick. Western Australia.
(ACTION) SCOTT AICHNER (PORTRAIT) CLAUDIO KIRAC

joel parkinson

His pedigree bloodline is as pure as his surfing. Joel rides with a powerful elegance inherited directly from his legendary uncle Darryl. Happy-go-lucky, hilarious, filled with joy, Joel has emerged as a whole new force, a whole new philosophy on the pro tour. Radical, expressive, fast yet strangely delicate, Joel's surfing is Kelly squared. A master at everything: aerials, tuberiding, carving 360's, you name it, his spontaneous, yet seamless, approach uses every opportunity a wave will give. And then Joel will give back his own, elevating his performance into something both grounded and ephemeral.

World title? Surely. It's just a matter of time. Built for this, born for this life both physically and philosophically, Joel wears the pride of all Australia and its hopes for another world champion easily. It's easy for him because in many ways, Joel is Australia. A new Australia. Beleaguered underdog no more, no Aussie battler for him, his confidence as a world power comes organically, blessed by the country he loves. Born on the beach, raised in perfect spinning barrels with his mates, loving every minute of his life, Joel represents the quality of a young man who found his element and then chose to live in it.

A competitive phenomenon, his pro career is a given. Guaranteed success. A sure bet. But then that's not all he is. Community minded, he gives back with countless appearances at surf schools. Already serving as an inspiration before his time has barely begun. It's in his blood. The Australian way. Secretly an avid designer, his theories on plan shapes, bottom contours and fin design baffle all but his favourite shaper.

Yes, Joel's story is yet to be told, but what an opening chapter. Already a champion threat. Hawaiian big-wave credentials paid for and established, winner of ASP titles. His will be a book that one cannot put down. A future, the future that stretches out before us all will be not only shared, but led by Joel Parkinson. Few surfers have achieved this: Carroll, Curren, Occy, Kelly, but none with quite the easygoing joy that Joel possesses.

It is a facet of his personality that serves him, and us, best. His is no inner angst-driven mission for recognition or protection against private self-recriminations and demons. His is not some overwhelming desire to rattle his sabres and beat down the enemy. Joel's mission is more of a reflection of what it can mean to be good at something, good at heart and from a good place.

Though still a work in progress, the world awaits Joel's final art. And with laughter and exuberance and a beautiful country in his soul, Joel is painting masterpieces with every wave he rides. **– Matt George.**

jack mccoy

Jack McCoy started making surf films back in the mid-'70s and has since become the best in the business. His movies succeed in doing what very few surf films do – inspire both hardcore surfers and the highbrow art world alike. So many surf films are regarded by outside the sport types as repetitive, narrativeless drivel, in the same league as porno. McCoy's films bring in such elements as storyline, humour, superb shots and wicked soundtracks, all of which combine to capture the attention of, well, pretty much everyone. "The guy who really kicked it off for me in film was Wayne Lynch," says McCoy, flashing back on his career. "He's the one who taught me to be a perfectionist. 'If you're going to do it, do it right,' he used to say… I'm really hard on myself, but as I get older I'm learning to not beat myself up about it. If I didn't get it, it didn't happen."

McCoy's films present surfing as an all-encompassing, spiritual pursuit with a huge emphasis on the surfers' personalities, which consequently has ruffled more than a few feathers. But this hasn't slowed him down in the slightest. "I make no apologies for wanting to do things right," McCoy says. "Admittedly, I have a much higher image of these guys than they have. Ultimately it's about me making them look good… But some of them don't really get it. I've had 'em say to me 'What's running round a tree have to do with making a surf film?'" In the case of McCoy's vision, running around a tree can be the shot that links or disconnects two similar or entirely different scenes, something that's clear in his head but often weird to the surfers. But one thing's for sure. He puts his time in and does his homework. And his love of his subjects is unrivalled. "I don't think you can make a decent surf film without understanding your talent," explains McCoy. "Any director will tell you he studies the work of the person he's going to work with. To film someone you need to know them, to understand them. When I'm working with a surfer I've never worked with before, I always try to watch him surf a little bit beforehand, see where he does his turns, see where he likes to go on the wave. 'Cause when I'm in the water I need to know instinctively what the hell he's likely to do next."

As a result of knowing his surfers inside and out, McCoy manages to nail shots so succinctly that you feel like you're right there with the rider, immersed in the aqua waters of some north-west reef break or barrelled off your nuts at Teahupo'o. This doesn't come easy. In fact, there's something going on here that's more intuitive than rational. For example, McCoy has had an uncanny knack for working with the Next Big Surfer before the rest of the world catches on. Cases in point: Wayne Lynch, Kong, Margo, Rasta, even Andy Irons. "I grew up watching Ricky Grigg, Peter Cole, Fred Van Dyke," he explains. "You knew that when Jock Sutherland was coming up and Jeff Hakman was coming up, they were going to be the next guys that were going to step in line. And then Gerry Lopez. And then Reno. And then when I'd go back to Australia you could see guys like Nat, Ted Spencer, Wayne Lynch were going to be the next talents. I just like to think I know a good surfer when I see one."

McCoy knows good surfers, there's no doubt about this. He also knows good waves, light, colour, composition, and timing – which are a few core ingredients he's turned into his trademark. But we mustn't leave good times out of the picture, because above all else, this is what McCoy cares about most. **– Jamie Brisick.**

Jack McCoy, photographed by Jamie
Brisick, North Shore winter, 2002/03.

michael 'munga' barry

Gold Coast kid arrives on the late '80s scene with a smooth, swooping style and a lot of heart. Goes to Hawaii for the first time and charges like a bull. Reputation shoots through the roof. Respect on all fronts. But what gets overshadowed by all the big-wave glory is what this kid can do in the small stuff. Munga is a machine. His hips never stop swaying; his board never stops S-ing. And then there's this knack for finding the tube that seems to sprinkle its way into heats. Munga kicks arse through the '90s. A fantastic competitive career that proved itself on every level. Think Munga and you think of a gloriously late Sunset Beach take-off, widow's peak style, the entire Pacific Ocean in an A-frame. Long, sweeping bottom turn and even longer textbook frontside carve at J-Bay. Six-foot sloppy onshore peaks and Munga in the tube at Hossegor. Contest victories. Adventures in foreign lands. And who can forget McCoy's footage of him in WA – hellish right barrel, a few times overhead – Munga in the tube, standing tall. A big man in a little man's body on a big wave with little room for screw-ups.

Munga's a gentleman. His reputation in the surfing world has as much to do with him as a person as it does with his waveriding. The fact that he started the Godfathers Foundation is as important as his victory in the '98 Billabong/MSF Pro at J-Bay. Him banding together a bunch of top pros to donate boards to underprivileged kids is as cool as him standing in a triple-overhead barrel somewhere south of Perth, among sharks and sharp reefs and no medical help for miles. And the giving back doesn't stop here. For the last couple of years, Munga has served as contest director for the Billabong Pro at J-Bay. The Gold Coast kid takes the reins and ensures that the contestants get the fairest shake in the finest possible surf. Walking the walk translated to an A-grade WCT event.

In pro surfing, the glory years are generally from early-20s to mid-30s. After that it's about much more than how hard you can hit the lip or how high you placed in the last contest. Many of the greats go down as merely guys who were able to stand up on surfboards exceptionally well, and nothing more. But with Munga there's something much bigger going on. He's got class, integrity, and a generous heart. And while he continues to tear the bag out of it as far as his surfing goes, it's Munga the Man who rises tall in the grand scheme of things. **– Jamie Brisick.**

Munga's finest celluloid moment, dropping late and critical into a Sunset Beach peak.

(ACTION) ART BREWER (PORTRAIT) AITIONN

47

taj burrow

Taj Burrow does a good American drawl. Pulling up at the drive-thru of a Taco Bell at Huntington Beach, he leans out the window and says, "Uh, ah'm gonna need, uh, lahk a case-a-dear, an enshee-lada, uh you got hart sauce for that? Uh, and a…" You get the idea. The drive-thru chick understands him perfectly, which never would have happened if he'd used his native Australian drawl. With a smirk, he picks up his lunch from the counter and drives on. Then he starts to wonder what it would be like if this little charade had actually been his whole life. It could have, easily.

Taj's oldies split from California before he was born, resettling in Margaret River, where they raised their precious only child in a more mellow community, near less crowded, more powerful waves. "Imagine if my parents had decided to stay," he says. "I'd be doing these promos (Taj has just released a new surfing instruction book), and the talk-up would be like, 'What about a big shout out for my new book, huh? TB's in the house, y'all! Yeeooooow!'"

It's not that Taj is down on the US. But like all kids who are comfortable in their skin, he just thinks where he grew up is best. And when you compare the down-home year-round comfort of Margs to the mid-summer hype of Huntington, well… there's no contest. "You can't tell what this place is like until you get out," he says. "I think my parents would have gotten to Australia and gone, 'Whoa, that joint was heavy'." How heavy? During the comp, a little blonde girl, about eight years old, comes up to him and says, "My mommy says you're my daddy. Is that true?" Taj calls her bluff. Her "mom" appears, and admits to being the girl's older sister. But, for a moment, she gets what thousands of young women on that beach want: Taj's attention. Yeah, he loves the US, but grow up there? Maybe not…

Taj was marked for stardom early, even by surfing's standards. Taj practiced airs, reverses and their variations until they were second nature. This was long before the rest of a nation obsessed with rail-turns cottoned on to the fact that airs weren't the reserve of weak surfers and that they were simply part of surfing's progression. His reef surfing was sharpened in the waves of Western Australia's south-west and, each winter, his parents, both good, keen surfers, would uproot and go surfing in the Indonesian-style lefts of the north-west. When other Australian kids dreamed of following Luke Egan, Matt Hoy and Munga Barry, Taj put his stake on the Momentum Generation: Kelly Slater, Shane Dorian, Rob Machado.

Taj blitzed the Billabong Junior Series and the WQS in the same year, seeded himself for a launch into the top of the 'QS and qualified for the 'CT the next year, all before he turned 19. Then he did a remarkable thing. He declined the invitation to join the Top 44. The dream of every young competitor in the world, and he was saying no to it. Why? Simple. He didn't feel ready. Surfing for a stake in history against Slater, Machado and their ilk could wait. He had some growing up to do first. And he wanted to study his own surfing in fine detail.

Probably no surfer in history has watched himself surf as much as Taj. He's serious about it, looking for flaws or missed opportunities to pull off big moves. And now, rated three in the world, he dreams of ditching it all to make the greatest surf film ever. Not comp surfing, real surfing, pushing the boundaries. Maybe then we'll see what the kid's really capable of. **– Sam McIntosh.**

kevin jones

Kevin Jones is an enigma. But though it is hard to get a comprehensive interview out of him, he takes the sport of snowboarding and its related business very seriously. He enters few contests in a season and yet when he does he brings home the results. And he is one of the few professional riders who is willing and able to balance filming commitments with competitions. Not bad for a lad who, by his own admission, was a teenage thorn in his parents' side.

Born in Sacramento, California, in 1975, Kevin gravitated to the dark side and soon became the stereotypical West Coast skater punk. Snowboarding, in its neon, rather camp, formative years was not a sport that would instantly appeal to such an urchin of the ply. But after checking Noah Salaznek and John Cardiel tear up the Grind skatepark and having watched the cult snowboard movie Riders on the Storm, Kevin was converted. He now lives full time in the heartland of American freestyle rippers, Mammoth Lakes, California.

Kevin's riding story is one of success of Donald Trump proportions. His clutch of sponsors reads like a kid's most wanted Christmas list. It includes Jeenyus, Billabong, Von Zipper, Northwave Drake, DVS shoes, TSG, and Level gloves by whom he is not only sponsored but also has several pro-models; an indication of his popularity among the riding masses. It is also no surprise then that he has appeared with monotonous frequency on the Transworld Rider Polls.

Although contests are not Kevin's primary concern, when he does enter them he invariably takes home the accolades for his troubles. His nine gold medals in both big air and slopestyle at the X Games are a testament to his success and make him the most decorated male athlete in the history of the games. He also boasts consecutive wins at two of the most prestigious stateside jib contests, the Nixon Jibfest and the Sims World's. These successes are surely proof enough that Kevin rips, but if still unconvinced check out his antics in movies past and present, including the latest release from Fourstar Distribution, Video Gangs. As if all this was not enough, from a business perspective, Kevin has found time to form one of snowboarding's newest and most irreverent snowboard brands, Jeenyus, for whom he also rides and has a pro-model.

So, what does a guy with so much on his plate do to chill out? Fish, of course! Kevin is an obsessive fisherman of the flyfishing persuasion and even competed in the ESPN Great Outdoors Games in 2002 for fishing. But, beware, don't get him started on tales of angling. The punk'll talk you to death.

All things considered, it is no wonder that his contemporaries heap praise on him, including Jussi Oksanen who said: "The bastard can do everything too good". **– Danny Burrows.**

Kevin Jones and the magic that happens when a world-class athlete meets a twist of snowpark metal.

(ACTION) JEFF BAKER (PORTRAIT) DANNY ZAPALAC

tara dakides

You see that wash of reptilian colour from lower back to torso? It's the prize adornment on the body of Tara Dakides, snowboarding super-hero. A woman who busted her back and was temporarily paralysed the first time she attempted a backflip; yet five years, and innumerable hours of practice, later she blew away any semblance of competition from her female peers when she nailed a flip clean at the '98 Vans Triple Crown. "I feel comfortable inverted," she once joked in one of her many appearances in Transworld magazine.

What's her story? Tara grew up around gymnastics and skateboards, but split from the family crib at 16 midway through her parent's divorce and moved to the Californian mountain town of Mammoth Lakes. Soon, she was racking up an endless list of podium placements across the sports disciplines of slopestyle, quarter and pipe; a winning streak that included five gold medals at the X Games. She even won a motocross event in 1997, although this is a passion that she has more recently put on a backburner.

Her list of accolades does not end with contest results though: Sports Illustrated named her "one of the coolest women in sports", while she was a nominee in the women's category of Laureus World Sports Awards in 2001. That year she received four awards at the Transworld Riders Poll – riders' choice, SIA retailers' choice, best female rail rider and best female freerider – and was nominated for a further four the following year. She even has groupies. Young men scrawl TARA on their chests and scream 'emselves hoarse at events. Boys propose marriage.

Life sure is good for Tara, but she has laboured long and hard for her rewards. Through her committed riding she has earned a pro-model at her new sponsors Jeenyus, a Vans boot, a signature line with Billabong, a signature goggle and sunglasses with Von Zipper along with a signature helmet with Pro-Tec, and mainstream sponsors Mountain Dew and Campbells soup.

What else? She's into raising money for breast cancer; digs surfing and owns a house in the southern Californian town of Oceanside. Is into photography, art, music, design, fashion, decor, has been involved in two video games and has her own X Games commercial. Tara's even had an action figure made of herself.

But not only is she financially savvy and secure, she also has creative inclinations and writes prose and poetry incessantly. Are there no limits to the talents and achievements of this lass? **– Danny Burrows.**

Physically and athletically, Tara Dakides is without peer: grinding into the sun, giving the reptile a little air beside the pool.

(ACTION) IAN RUHTER (PORTRAIT) SCOTT NEEDHAM/SNP5000.COM

axel pauporte

Axel's destiny was to become a lawyer, not some heroic Big Mountain rider. In fact, his whole involvement in the sport of snowboarding has been a contradiction. Born in Brussels, the son of a lawyer and a school teacher, the expanse of surrounding flatlands was a serious hitch to his pursuit of mountain sports. But "not being a city kind of guy" he brought back from family holidays the art of snowboarding which he was to vigorously practice on the dry slopes of Belgium. At first he thought he had joined the sport too late to progress in it, judging by the riding that he had seen and this being the '80s, but he was soon sponsored by the regional distributors of Burton and Gotcha and cadging rides to the mountains two or three times a year.

His real break though came in Val D'Isere where he spent his first two seasons and where he crossed paths with Regis Roland, who was in the process of creating A snow-boards. Regis took the young Belgian onto his team, installing him at Les Arcs in the French Alps. It was here, with the help of skillful guiding from Regis, that Axel moved away from his dryslope-inspired freestyling and nurtured his passion for the backcountry. It was here too that he first caught a glimpse of his vision of snowboarding in the form of Steve Graham: "The biggest influence on my snowboarding was Steve Graham. He was the ultimate rider. A really strong new school freestyler who was doing new tricks in the backcountry." Axel's big mountain freestyle is a legacy of this meeting.

Axel was soon making good money out off his passion of filming across the globe, and it was on celluloid by the likes of Justin Hostynek that he forged his reputation as a back-country rider with balls of steel. From Odd Man Out to the latest Hostynek movie, Saturation, he has had audiences tearing the stuffing out of their sofas as he spins cliffs that most mortals would not dare to straight jump. Ironic really, that while he inspires others through his movie appearances, movies from a voyeurs perspective are one of his greatest passions. "I love movies and buying DVDs. I would love to watch every movie that there has ever been." He rates Reservoir Dogs in his top five movies but holds a special place in his film obsession for Man Bites Dog, which was filmed in the neighbourhood where he grew up.

In true film-o-phile style he recently married his heli-pilot wife in Las Vegas, complete with Elvis and a honeymoon in Hawaii. But this was no shotgun, B-movie scene. This is the real deal – forever more etc. Axel and Flora now spend much of their time at their house in Hossegor surfing, playing golf and riding motorbikes.

But in the minds of his fans, the steeps will always be Axel's terrain park, especially Alaska, and after such choice pickings he has become choosy where and when he now rides. Not to say that he no longer enjoys riding, as he does with friends and when the conditions are right, but in his own words: "Once you have travelled first class it's hard to go back to economy". **– Danny Burrows.**

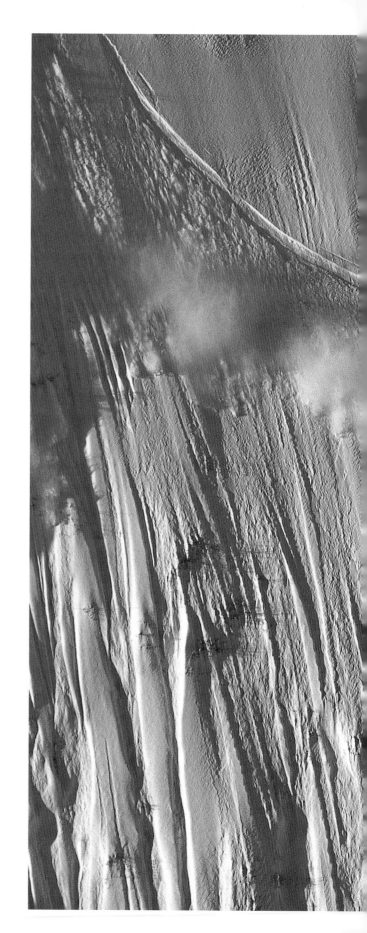

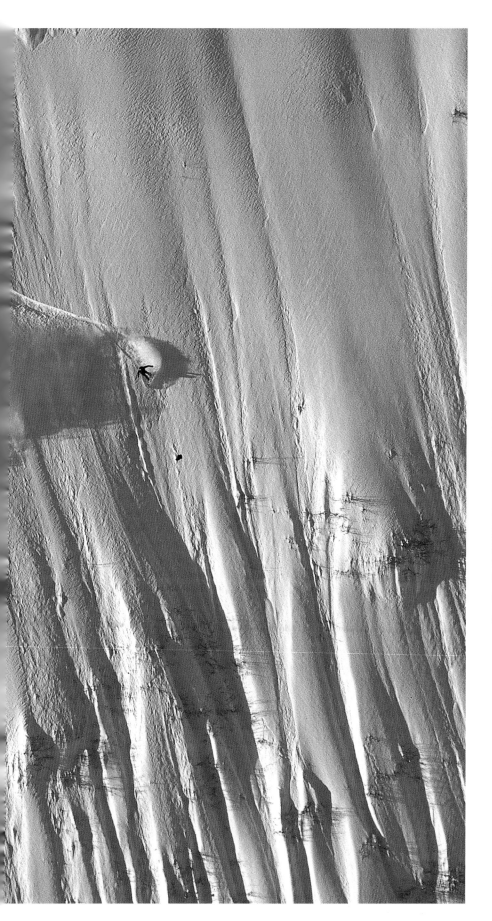

The purest of White Lines. Axel Pauporte, married to a helicopter pilot, living a somewhat fantastic dream way out of bounds.

(ACTION) FLORENT DUCASSE (PORTRAIT) BRUSTI

Bucky, ruling a bowl of flames in Algorta, Spain.

TIMO JARVINEN

bucky lasek

It was April 1990 and Bucky stood ready, fresh-faced, 18-years-old, and with a long career as a pro ahead of him. He was at the Edge Skatepark, in Fremantle, Western Australia, doing a demo with Tony Hawk and Frankie Hill. Bucky was amped to land his first 720 that night. He started spinning them no problem and even laid a couple down. On his final attempt he over-rotated on the re-entry and fell 12 foot backwards to the flat. The deafening sound that followed wasn't the kind of noise you want to hear a human make. The whiplash Bucky sustained was phenomenal. There was a point where the back of his head was touching the middle of his back. He somehow peeled himself off the flat bottom and slithered to the back of the park. Lying on a dysfunctional ramp, Bucky was left to fend off signature-gathering fans and explain why he didn't want to give out any stickers. At this point, any-one about to embark on a pro career might have had second thoughts, but not Bucky. He has since become one of the world's most innovative and consistent vert skaters, and is still revealing a new trick at each public appearance.

Bucky was born and raised in Baltimore, and being a vertical connoisseur on the east coast of America during the '80s was no easy task. There was plenty of weather dodging and driving and dedication needed. The timing of Bucky's assault on the pro vert ranks was impeccably bad: vert was about to die in the arse. The early-'90s were a dark era for skateboarders all around. While everyone flicked around their paddle pop boards with micro-sized wheels, they forgot about vert skating. The mags stopped running vert in their editorial and the companies stopped paying vert riders. Luckily for Bucky, he has always been able to skate everything and still shone during this quiet time.

In the mid-late '90s, skating was again growing in epidemic proportions and Bucky was one of the main players aboard Tony Hawk's Birdhouse Skateboards. In 1999, Birdhouse dropped their legendary video: The End. Tony was about to retire from the contest circuit and in The End he handed over the reins to Bucky, who was freshly repaired from knee surgery and ready to go off. Bucky's calm during a vert comp remains unparalleled. His ability to relax in the most stressful circumstances is uncanny.

In the past four years, Bucky has won over 10 World Cup contests and five gold medals, has been featured in Rolling Stone magazine and has mastered tricks that no one has even landed before. He is the only pro who can do switch 540s… in his run! In July 2003, Bucky won the world's richest-ever skating event: the Boost Mobile Pro and backed it up with gold medals at both the X Games and Gravity Games – the most successful year for any skater in the history of vert skating.

When he is not suspended over the world in a plane or on a skateboard, Bucky lives in Carlsbad, California with his wife Jennifer and his two daughters. **– Morgan Campbell.**

European vert champ Terence Bougdour likes his ramps big, his days long, his boats fast and his McDonalds warm and frequent.

ALL PHOTOS NICOLAS MALINOWSKI

terence bougdour

Terence is 25, been riding pro since he was 18, recently won his second consecutive European vert title, was voted Etnies rider of the year, lives up there in the French Alps and rounds out his life by singing in a punk band. This interview with Terence Bougdour was recorded in the autumn of 2003...

Your greatest moment in skating?
Up to this day, it's my first McTwist at the Vans Skate Park in Orange County, Southern California. I'd been working for ages on this trick so when I made it… it was a great time!

How does skating affect your life?
I get up late and go to bed late. I get to meet lots of different people. It's like I have two lives, at home with my close crew of friends and my girlfriend and then, when I compete, I meet different people. Skateboarding is my job but unlike many people, I really like my job.

Talk me through an average day...
Get up around 10am, video games, e-mail sessions, wakeboarding, or riding boats or swimming on the lake, skateboarding for a couple of hours, then the gym, then back home… you want to know the rest? When I am competing, it's more routine – contests, McDonalds and TV! I skate a couple of hours every day of the week and I usually skate at home. I am lucky to have a ramp at home that we (the skate club created by Terence, Florent Viard and the ABS skate shop) have just renovated. We are also working on a new project to build a bigger ramp closer to the lake of Annecy, with billboards for sponsors and stuff. We have great connections with the city of Annecy, we work with the mayor, but it is a bit hard to find a place to put the ramp as long as it is going to involve advertising money. The skate club is our way to create the structure we need to skate.

Describe your equipment?
… a skateboard, pair of shoes, surf boardshorts and protection gear… I usually need a couple of each per month, and even more boardshorts 'cause nylon rips off easily on the ramp…

Signature trick?
The Frog Air! It's like a Superman in FMX or BMX – sort of lying in the air with the board against my stomach and legs apart. Just like a French frog.

Interview by Christel Dupiellet.

Skateboarding's internationalist Chad
Bartie, b/s tailslide over the pool light.

(ACTION) BURNETT (PORTRAIT) TIMO JARVINEN

chad bartie

AC/DC riffs blare out over the expanse of the Ostrov Stvanice Island and off into the winding streets of Prague. It has been a year to the day since this quaint setting has been injected with this kind of energy. The reason: Chad Bartie is beginning his run on the Mystic Cup street course. His lanky frame and wide gait are reaching the maximum speed that is attainable on such a course. Within seconds he covers the entire width of the park: down the bank, up the pyramid, ollie the pyramid, up the next bank, up a road barrier, backside tailslide the barrier and back down eight feet of banks onto the course. His signature black mop of hair barely seems to keep up. Forty seconds later, his run is over and he has hit 12 different obstacles and landed every single trick with absolute ease and finesse. As he dismounts, his face erupts into his widest grin, one of genuine enjoyment. Unlike the other pros, Chad is in Prague without a board or a shoe sponsor – Billabong clothing his only supporter – but has still made a point of hitting all the Euro comps. Anyone else in such sponsorship limbo would have stayed home, but Bartie is about to score second place.

Chad's roots as a master of all things outdoor were formed on Australia's Gold Coast where he was born 26 years back. As a kid, Chad would spend any given week juggling trail-bike riding, BMX, surfing and skating. It was his skating that stood out and he embarked on an epic pro career. His mum Joan, his father Dave (who was a motocross champion), and brother Jamie have always supported Chad's skating: he has had a back-yard ramp since the age of eight. Growing up on the Gold Coast has allowed Chad access to all types of terrain, from the schoolyards of the GC to the rugged imperfections of the infamous Pizzey Bowl.

Where most of today's street pros concentrate on one facet of street skating: rails or stairs, Chad is ridiculously well-rounded. He has something for every possible obstacle in his path.

At 15, Chad visited the US with his sidekick Matt Mumford. It was here that the spark for professional skate-dom finally embedded itself deep in his psyche. After a five-month stay in the coastal town of Encinitas (San Diego County), Chad returned to Oz and received a model on Kewday Skateboards. Two years later, and Chad had pages of coverage under his belt and had turned the head of many a visiting American pro. Much to the disappointment of his teenage sweetheart, Hannah, it was time again for Chad to head back to the States. For the next few years he would alternate between the beach areas of San Diego and the Gold Coast, spending six months in each locale. During this time, the varied terrain that Chad would hit was having an incredible effect on his skill levels.

In 1999, a successful visa application allowed Chad to make the move to California, and his wife Hannah would soon follow. Over the past five years he has been living the dream life of international exploration as a pro skater. And despite a couple of nasty ankle injuries and sponsorship hiccups he remains with his feet firmly planted on his griptape, focused and on the mission. His humble approach towards his career is obviously one of the reasons he has sustained his dream for so long. Chad reflects: "My dream was to travel the world through skateboarding and the only way to do it was by turning pro. So I wanted to come back and try and do it. And, if I didn't do it, that's cool. I just gave my hardest effort and it paid off." – **Morgan Campbell.**

THE ☀ FEELING

"SURFING MAKES ME FEEL LIKE I'M PART OF THE BIGGER PICTURE. WHEN I'M BY MYSELF AND THE WATER'S CLEAN AND THE DAY IS BEAUTIFUL THERE'S NO OTHER PLACE I'D RATHER BE AT THAT POINT. I SOMETIMES FIND MYSELF FEELING THAT, LITERALLY, THIS IS THE BEST THING I COULD BE DOING ON EARTH." SHANE DORIAN

SHANE DORIAN / HIGH SPEED REBOUND / INDONESIA 63

TED GRAMBEAU

Jamie Sterling learned to surf under the eye of Hawaii's Ronnie Burns – his mother Tina was engaged to Ronnie at the time of his death in 1990. Only 10 when Ronnie died, Jamie says he feels his presence in big waves, and says he got a little push from his step-dad during the 2003 Hansens Energy Pipe Pro. "It was big, true Pipe," remembers Jamie. "I knew he loved Pipe at that size. And that day, everything was easy, everything was auto-matic. He was on my shoulder. He was living through my experience." Of surfing, Jamie says it gives him a "clear mind, a sense of direction – it brings out my creativity. It makes me think a lot clearer when I surf a lot."

BRIAN BIELMANN

HAWAII'S JAMIE STERLING / DRIVEN BY THE SPIRIT OF RONNIE BURNS / PIPELINE / FEBRUARY 2003

PIPELINE

"I like to grab my rail so I can hold my speed without spinning out, without taking one in the melon. Every carve I try and make as fast and hard as I can," says Benji. "Surfing is pure freedom, sounds corny, but it's the only pure thing left, right? Especially in California, it's the only thing that can stop you feeling like a full-on weirdo."

JASON CHILDS

BENJI WEATHERLY/
PART OF THE ORIGINAL MOMENTUM GENERATION/
B'S GRABRAIL CARVE/
NORTH SHORE/.
HAWAII

65

"I love backside airs," says Hawaii's Jason Shibata. "They're so much different to frontside airs – the whole motion, the longer, more drawn-out line you take to the lip. I love that moment of anticipation just before you boost."

PETE HODGSON

HAWAIIAN JASON SHIBATA / BJS 180 /
NORTH SHORE /
OAHU

LUKE EGAN / PACIFIC
TAHITI /
FRENCH POLYNESIA

HYPNOSIS /

A rising swell on a lay day during the 2003 Billabong Pro. Luke's out with Occy and Kelly Slater and the swell's on the rise outta the west. For one hour it turns on and the three have the heavy inside wrap to themselves, taking turns and threading their way through wide-open barrels. Jack McCoy's shooting for Blue Horizon and claims he's got some of his best clips for the film. It's testimony to surfing's enduring pull that Luke, with nearly three decades of surfing under his belt, is still moved by the simple act of riding waves. "I've surfed for a long time now and I've surfed a lot of good waves. I love that exhaustion from surfing all day because it means the surf's been really good. Doing that body check at night knowing you've done three surfs."

SEBASTIAN ROJAS

Coolangatta's Joel Parkinson, competing in a semi-final during a WQS event near Lagundi Bay on the island of Nias. The event had been cursed with flat surf for most of the waiting period and the decision was made to locate to a reef ledge three km down the beach. Exposed to swell, the surfers were faced with eight foot tubes – a high barrel out back coming into a terrifying hole toward the end. You know things are serious when the hands of the world's most relaxed surfer are suffering a palsy in the throat of a doubling Indonesian cave. Joel backdoored this and emerged screaming, arms raised in triumph.

SIMON WILLIAMS

"Whenever you surf Teahupo'o it's orgasmic, it's an orgasm every time you ride a wave like that," says Andy Irons, pictured here on a wave photographers in the channel labelled the Black Death. "How do you come off the bottom off a wave like that? It's instinct. You're frozen with fear. It's all total reaction. It's the adrenalin. As I got caught up in the lip I thought about jumping off and trying to get through the back but there's no way it would've let me go so I had to follow through. Then you feel the fire hose. When you feel that spit you know you've done the right thing."

TOM SERVAIS

ANDY IRONS /RACE WITH THE DEVIL /
TEAHUPO'O

Andy and the world title chair at Sunset Beach. A week later, post-celebration, he's in the final event of the season, the Pipe Masters. Focussed, he takes out his fourth event win of the season and picks up the Triple Crown.
STEVE SHERMAN

ANDY IRONS / THE SWEETEST RIDE /
SUNSET BEACH

KAIEWA MEYER

72

In the early '90s when bodyboarding was at its frenzied peak, Billabong's support of it was seen by some in the surfing community as a contentious move. Now that the furore has died down, it seems they were just a lot more clear-eyed than those at the extremes of that debate. It's not what you want to be doing at Huntington or Bells, but Pipe's a skate park to these guys, and there's no arguing with the contribution the prone contingent made when they first discovered and rode the slabs of Teahupo'o. These days, anywhere there's a wave that sucks below sea level, there's a bunch of crazy local bodyboarders who just dig getting deep barrels.

It's no surprise that Billabong's bodyboarding team is the strongest in the world and has been for around 10 years. In fact, bodyboarding delivered Billabong its first world champion: Michael 'Eppo' Eppelstun, Australia's only bodyboarding world champ so far. Eppo threw together weird combos like a skateboarder, invented the ARS (air-roll-spin), the double roll and the backflip, and was the first Australian bodyboarder to win at Pipe. The rest of the team are equally worthy.

Dave Ballard's a Cronulla local who's just as happy at the Point on his surfboard as he is trimming through horror pits at Shark Island on his sponge. As one of Australia's drop-knee pioneers, Dave was influential in making Australian kids see that there was more to life than just riding on your belly.

Ryan Hardy's from a hardcore Margaret River surfing family (twin brother Brett and older brother Gene have both scored magazine covers and their dad Tony is well-respected in the Margaret River lineup) and took his prone act to the reefs of the world, winning the first-ever bodyboard contest at Teahupo'o in 12-foot plus bombs. He's a four-time winner of Riptide mag's Peer Poll and one of Australia's most influential boarders.

Andre Botha entered his first Pipe contest at age 15, won the world title there at 17, and backed it up the following year with another Pipe win and another world title. The South African has been chasing huge tubes around the world ever since, and took what is easily the heaviest wipeout ever recorded at Teahupo'o, falling some 20 feet out of the lip (pictured at right). It took him a while to laugh about that one...

BILLY MORRIS
DAVE BALLARD / ON THE KNEE / TAHITI

ANDRE BOTHA / AIR REVERSE / PIPELINE
TIM JONES

JOE LIBBY
EPPO / INVERTED AIR / OFF THE WALL

ANDRE BOTHA / LATE DIVE / TEAHUPO'O
IAN STEWART

"TAG A TRUNK"

BOARDSHORTS:
Billabong

TAG A TRUNK / INK / GOLD COAST

SCOTT NEEDHAM/SNP5000.COM

Billabong introduced the world to custom boardshorts via 2002's tag-a-trunk advertising campaign. Surfers bought blank white boardshorts and, either with supplied stencils or at their own whim, used paint to create unique one-off shorts. During the photo shoot, participants took more than a little delight in showering each other with buckets of paint. Taj Burrow, Andy Irons, Shane Dorian, tagged.

BRIAN GRUBB/ WAKE SKATE KICK FLIP /
BYLEY'S HOUSE /
ORLANDO
FLORIDA

"It's totally involving, it's a total release," Brian says of wakeskating, listing the ability to nail shuv-its and kickflips as advantages over strapped-in wakeboarding. Smaller boards, no bindings and the traction afforded by wearing shoes, says Brian, means even wilder tricks.

JOEY MEDDOCK

(Right) The first time the multiple Canadian champ hit this 35-foot road gap he left the up ramp early, hit the road, and bounced into a stack of bricks. Says Chad, "I got real lucky, just cuts and scrapes. At the last minute I threw a helmet on. It saved my head." Chad sessioned this gap 15 times that day and lives for wakeboarding because, "there's a real freedom out there to do whatever you want, jump or slide. And there's escape, because even if you're having a crappy day you'll still be having fun."

JOSHUA LETCHWORTH

CHAD SHARPE /
STRAPPED GAP JUMP / THE PROJECTS /
ORLANDO FLORIDA

"Making a manoeuvre like this, it's enlightenment. Your emotions run free, you're happy, you're free. You've stepped up, you've reached the highest point, you've made one of the most radical turns ever. You're high and you're ready to go again…" Dylan Longbottom, riding his brother's first-ever surfboard, a 5'7" Gordon and Smith twin-fin, made in 1980.

SIMON WILLIAMS

DYLAN LONGBOTTOM /
STRAPPED INVERTED REVERSE /
INDONESIA

"Being strapped inside a tube is friggen terrifying – you're so committed to making the barrel. Eat it and you gotta hope you don't blow your ankles or knees out," says Snips. "But, with straps, you can ride the foamball and hit obstacles when normally you'd be thrown off. It's a risky business, for sure."

TOM SERVAIS

MIKE PARSONS / STRAPPED TUBE /
TEAHUPO'O

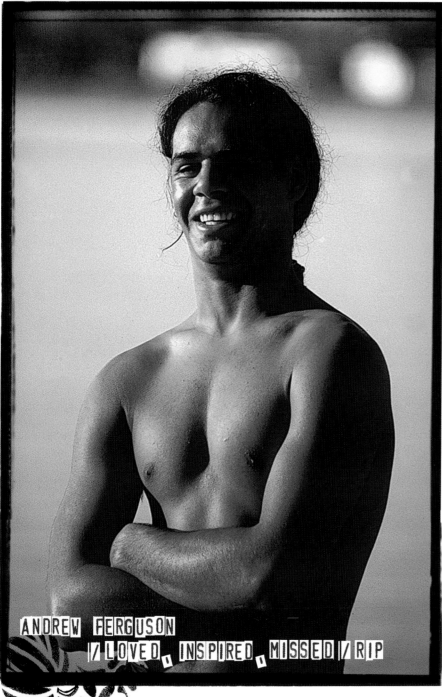

ANDREW FERGUSON
/ LOVED , INSPIRED , MISSED / RIP

The exchange of cultures became far more important than the accumulation of points and the deciding of heat winners.

Traditional painting for the contest poster.

INDIGENOUS INVITATIONAL BILLABONG

Scott Rotumah, a winner in '96 and '98.

ALL PHOTOS JOLI

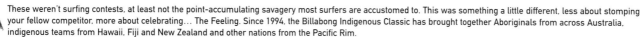

These weren't surfing contests, at least not the point-accumulating savagery most surfers are accustomed to. This was something a little different, less about stomping your fellow competitor, more about celebrating… The Feeling. Since 1994, the Billabong Indigenous Classic has brought together Aboriginals from across Australia, indigenous teams from Hawaii, Fiji and New Zealand and other nations from the Pacific Rim.

Former Billabong team manager Vince Lawder had a vision to develop and celebrate the surfing of Australian Aboriginals and give something back to a people that had been largely marginalised by white society. Press and television coverage was lavish, its praise generous. Something had begun to stir.

Helped by Robert "Bushy" Mitchell and Steve Williams, the Billabong Indigenous Classic identified dozens of previously unrecognised surfers and brought the depth of Aboriginal surfing to the fore. Goofyfooter Andrew Ferguson, from Coffs Harbour, soon became known as the Black Occ for his wild carves. When he died, aged 29, in 1999, WCT surfer Lee Winkler wrote: "I was overwhelmed by his presence… Aboriginal people have a very strong bonding – one big family. Ferg was one very special Koori, and without him knowing, his people had him mounted on their shoulders." Other strong talents included Josh Slabb, Ty Arnold, Scott Rotumah, Barry Chennall, Jacob Tippo, Rory Togo, Joe Hadden and the late Eric Mercy; a surfer, like Andrew Ferguson, who died in his prime. Each year, the most promising junior is awarded a carved didgeridoo – the Eric Mercy award. The Andrew Ferguson trophy is an encouragement award.

Unlike many of the big-money events, the Billabong Indigenous Classic moves people, touches souls. Many competitors, sudden friends, become blood brothers, cutting fingers and mixing blood. Says Bushy, who has run 756 contests over 20 years: "It's an experience money can't buy, a life experience. I'll take the friendships I made to the grave."

Taj first surfed this righthander when he was 11 years old, using it for tuberiding practice whenever a north-west swell and offshore easterly winds turned it on. Little did he realise that as the years passed this wave would become his aerial playground. Recently, Taj has used the wave to push the boundaries of aerial surfing. Pictured here, messing with a Superman before the tour kicked off in 2003. Says Taj, "Everyone always says, we need more time in the air, like motocross and BMX guys. More time would be a nice luxury, but we're doing fine. In surfing, we're all board and wind, so we've got to stop it flying away from our feet. Surfing's progressing quickly. Flips, Superman spins, they'll be like air reverses were five years ago."

TWIGGY

TAJ BURROW / SUPERMAN / SOUTH-WEST AUSTRALIA

SHANE DORIAN /
EYES ON THE CHANNEL / WAIMEA BAY /
HAWAII

Shane Dorian first surfed the Bay when he was 15, and became a regular the year after when he moved to the North Shore to live with big-wave obsessive's Brock Little and Todd Chesser. Both of whom would taunt the small teenager if he refused to join 'em out in the line-up of what was then regarded as the biggest rideable wave in the world. "By force I became comfortable out there," he says. When 2001's Eddie contest rolled around on Friday, January 12, 2001, the 28-year-old had been surfing Waimea for 13 years. Shane placed second to Ross Clarke-Jones and lists that result among his top accomplishments. "It was amazing, the day and competitively. The weather was gorgeous, the waves were big and clean and the sets were pumping."

JOHN BILDERBACK

FROM A RIPPLE TO A WAVE

MILESTONES IN THE INTERNATIONAL GROWTH OF |XXX| BILLABONG.

Jim Banks, Shark Island, Cronulla. Eight foot. Only one other surfer out, fellow Cronulla crazy Gerry Manion. What characterised Banks, apart from his travel wanderlust, was his commitment in reef waves from Voodoo and Shark Island in Australia to Uluwatu and Pipeline abroad.

PETER SIMONS

The story of how a bunch of surfers grew Billabong into the thriving global entity it is today is remarkable enough. That they did it without a skerrick of formal business training between them is astonishing.

The Billabong way has always been to grow in-house staff into positions of senior management over time – keenness and loyalty and a deep understanding of the market counting for more than business school credentials. "We just all had our education within Billabong," says Australian general manager Dougall Walker, one of Billabong's early team riders. "It's well acknowledged throughout the financial markets that our management team is very strong."

From the outset, Gordon and Rena surrounded themselves with a small team of key, trusted staff who understood their approach intimately. Gordon would always run everything on the smell of an oily rag. There weren't a lot of luxuries and Gordon would always put money straight back into the company. Employees grew Billabong with the understanding that there were no luxuries. Gordon had done it tough to get to where he was, and he expected others to do the hard yards too. He didn't like to communicate with too many different people in the organisation, to keep it really tight, so that one hand knew what the other hand was doing. It meant that key management people were working very long hours, but there were less communication breakdowns and hence less mistakes.

Providing opportunities for people to excel and be well-rewarded was also key. In the '80s, machinists on piece rates could earn many times the award wage if they were both fast and accurate. Sales agents, licensees and retailers have all grown with the company, sharing handsomely in the success and profits. "Gordon always said, 'I don't care if my business partners are making good money, because that means they're making me good money. Good business has got to be good for both parties'," says Dougall. He is proud of the fact that since 1986, annual turnover in Australia has grown from $7 million to $140 million, while retail customers have only increased from 600 to 650. "We haven't gone out and blown the whole thing out of the water. We've helped our business partners grow their businesses and we've both succeeded," says Dougall. "I can't think of any other business that's had that much organic growth through the same partners... After 30 years, a lot of our customers will let us write their orders, based on the data we've collected, on them and us, and help them move forward."

The stories of how key staff grew into their management roles, and how new markets were grown from the ground up, says a lot about the effectiveness of Billabong's self-styled form of surf commerce.

RENA MERCHANT 1973-1998
Before the famous Billabong triple-stitched boardshort, and nearly 20 years before kick-starting the girls division, Rena developed a thriving trade for her crocheted bikinis. All before her 21st birthday. Creative, driven and, like Gordon, able to adapt quickly to every single task of a clothing business, Rena combined the responsibilities of motherhood (three children) with her Gold Coast-Sydney monthly sales run, design, and the enormous stress of growing a business. Back in the early days, Gordon, Rena and the kids had to survive on $20 a week. $11 after they paid their weekly $9 rent. At the weekends the pair would set-up a stand at the Broadbeach flea markets and wholesale boardshorts for $4 apiece. Would Billabong be celebrating 30 years in business if Rena wasn't so closely involved? "Probably not," says Gordon. "She was an inspiration. During those times when we were close to bankrupt, Rena would hang tough, and say, 'We can grind our way out of this'. It takes courage to hang in there when everything looks bleak, when the bank won't give you another cent, when you're hundreds of thousands of dollars in debt. I'd wake up in the middle of the night in a lather of a sweat. Rena'd stay positive and say, 'Nothing will bring us down'." Rena, supported by assistants Heidi Bartholomew and Lorraine Anderson, was responsible for growing Billabong Girls to the point where it now accounts for a third of the company's revenue. A passionate advocate of the environment and sustainable living, Rena sold her 49 percent of the business in late 1999, prior to the company floating, and now lives on Queensland's Sunshine Coast.

COLETTE PAULL 1973-current
Gordon and Rena Merchant's personal assistant for many years, Colette has been a mainstay of the Billabong operation from the beginning. It's pretty clear without her the business wouldn't have thrived the way it did. She was the common sense Rock of Gibraltar in amongst the creativity of Gordon and Rena. In those early years, Colette handled everything from book keeping to legal issues, human resources to general trouble shooting. Although no longer directly employed by the company, she remains on the board of directors.

GREG WOODS 1981-2001
Greg started with Billabong in the early '80s and served as general manager for nearly 20 years. Greg oversaw the production side of the business, a key role in a company that was, at the time, primarily a manufacturing operation. At one point in the late '80s, Billabong employed 280 staff – 230 of them in manufacturing. Greg remained with the company until it was floated.

PETER CASEY 1984-current
Peter began as a machinist with Billabong when he was 17, straight out of school, when his mum lined up a summer holiday job for him.

He must have made a favourable impression on the ladies in the sewing room, because he was soon offered a full-time job. "Mum was a supervisor. She got me a job with Greg Woods, as a trainee manager," recalls Peter. "She said, 'If you get higher than a supervisor, I'm leaving,' and she did leave." Peter was largely responsible for taking Billabong production offshore, as head of what is now known as Central Sourcing. Peter set up Billabong's Hong Kong office 13 years ago, with a staff of one. Now, it employs 32 people in Hong Kong, eight people in Australia and a second office is being opened in mainland China with a dozen staff. "Central Sourcing is really there as a global catalyst to help people combine their production runs to achieve economies of scale," says Peter. "It allows Billabong to keep a tighter stranglehold on our branding and intellectual property so everything looks the same wherever in the world you may buy our product." In addition, Peter oversees international licensees and, in a support role to General Manager Dougall Walker, looks after Billabong's general operations in Australasia.

DOUGALL WALKER 1986-current
Dougall was Billabong's first sponsored team rider outside of Queensland, hailing from the competitive stronghold of Newport, on Sydney's northern beaches. "Thornton Fallander and Joe Engel used to stay at my house and they were sponsored by Billabong," Dougall explains. He was a finalist in the Pipeline Masters in Hawaii in 1980, and Australian champion in '82. He began working for Peak wetsuits and moved to California in 1985 to launch the brand in the US at a time when Billabong was starting to do well. He became friendly with then US licensee Bob Hurley and caught up with Gordon Merchant during his regular visits to California. "I was pretty much a physical wreck from working 18 hours a day," remembers Dougall. "Gordon said, 'Have you been surfing lately?' I remember him saying, 'You've got to go surfing, you've got to go surfing, it's the best de-stress tool.' And it worked." So well, in fact, that Dougall entered and won the US amateur titles in '85 – making him the only surfer with US and Australian national titles to his credit. When Dougall returned to Australia, Gordon offered him a job in his rapidly- expanding business as national head of sales and marketing. "I learnt a hell of a lot from Gordon. I was 26 years old when I started. I sat in his pocket for eight-to-10 years, that was my apprenticeship. From the mid-'90s on, he started to give me a lot more scope. You would have to earn your stripes before he would relinquish any responsibility of 'his baby'."

BRUCE TIPPETT 1980-current
A master salesman who cut his teeth in the cut-throat world of the jeans business of the late '70s. Bruce was the first sales agent employed by Billabong and was instrumental in not only expanding Billabong sales reach but was also a great sounding board for Gordon in product development.

Guy Ormerod, a brilliant goofyfooter, and a strong part of the Burleigh Heads movement in the '70s and '80s.

AITIONN

Bunyip Dreaming photo shoot (from left): Marcus Brabant, Ronnie Burns, Darren Magee, Munga Barry.

AITIONN

Thornton Fallander, a Burleigh stand-out and a star of Jack McCoy's seminal 1982 movie Storm Riders. Cyclone swell, 1987.

AITIONN

An early ad shoot for Billabong with Mark Occhilupo and Jim Banks. After a day of drinking and posing for the camera, the surfers and photographer Paul Sargeant wound up at Sarge's crib. Fooling around, the result was this classic image.

SARGE

VINCE LAWDER 1984-1999

Billabong's first team manager. Vince travelled the countryside signing up the hottest juniors to Billabong's surfer stable. He was such a popular figure with young surfers that he gained the nickname "Mr Whippy" because when he pulled up in a beach car park kids would come running!

TAKING IT TO THE WORLD

The nature of Billabong's business changed profoundly in the mid-'80s when the Australian government adopted the so-called Button plan, masterminded by Senator John Button, to reduce import duties and eliminate quotas on garments. This posed a huge challenge for the local industry. Gordon sat down his key employees and said, 'Our business has got to change'. The focus shifted from manufacturing to importing and helped create the environment for the rapid international expansion of the label. It helped the company to internationalise, and Billabong began exporting intellectual property, its designs and branding. And because the company started to develop an offshore manufacturing base that created export income, it helped to grow the business. Several key international markets grew rapidly through the mid-'80s.

THE USA

Gordon's affection for world-class surfing locales (he hasn't missed a Hawaiian winter in over 30 years) meant it was only a matter of time before Billabong was sold in the cradle of modern surfing, Hawaii and California. After promising sales in Hawaii, Gordon tested the water in California by supplying his boardshorts to the Encinitas Surf Shop, near San Diego. They sold out of a rack of boardshorts within a week and Gordon instantly knew there was a strong market for Billabong in the US. Entry into the market, however, did not come without its challenges. Californian surfer Chip Rowland teamed up with surfboard manufacturer Bob Hurley and between pooling his own savings, cash advances from Bob's brother, his relatives and Billabong in Australia, the company as a whole was put under a heavy fiscal burden. "We had to subsidise the kick-off for the first 18 months," says Gordon. "We had no security over the stock we shipped Bob or guarantees of cash in return. I just trusted Bob and his partners to do the right thing and they didn't let me down. My whole philosophy was to invest in the business today to look after the business tomorrow," says Gordon.

Bob Hurley became the driving force behind the label in the US, until the late '90s, when he left Billabong to start his own surf label. When he left in 1999, he took most of his staff and teamriders with him, and with the exception of sales manager Richard Sanders and his sales team, Billabong US had to be rebuilt almost from scratch. This provided a huge challenge, but also a great opportunity. "It gave us this huge advantage. We were able to handpick the A-team and restructure the company," says Gordon. Hurley stepped out with Billabong on a major ascent in the USA. Usually that kind of re-structuring is done because a business has fallen apart or gone into decline. Gordon ended up spending three months living at the Huntington Beach Hilton interviewing potential licensees. When it became clear that the task of finding a licensee to replace Bob's team was going to be too much of a compromise, Gordon decided that Billabong Australia would set up a new company and that he would find a CEO to run it.

While searching for a CEO one name kept cropping up: Paul Naude, a former Pipe Masters finalist, peer of the great Gerry Lopez and Rory Russell and an astute, dynamic businessman. "The aim of the game in the US," explains Naude, "is to stay at the forefront of innovation in the action sports industry." Naude and his talented staff haven't wasted time since taking over from Hurley and co. Projects driven from the US include 2000's zipperless wetsuit, the tag-a-trunk campaign, 2003's virtually stitchless Solution steamer, The Odyssey big-wave search, and the development of an edgier side to the company as a whole.

JAPAN

Japanese surf businessman Matsumoto and his partner Carma owned surfshops in Osaka before starting Billabong in Japan. The duo oversaw the growth of the Japanese market in the early-to-mid-'80s, importing Billabong product and eventually manufacturing some products under licence. Ultimately, as the market grew, Japan joined the Central Sourcing program. Then Carma went back into the surfshop game, while Matsumoto built the brand and guided growth until the mid-'90s, when he left Billabong. Billabong Japan's current CEO is talented surfer and expert businessman, Tetoshi Ueda.

SOUTH AFRICA

South Africa licensee Cheron Kraak is a legend of SA surfing and is known as the unofficial mayoress of Jeffreys Bay. Cheron is an extremely driven woman passionately involved in all aspects of the SA surf scene and took on Billabong in the early '80s. She already had her own successful label, Country Feeling, and later ran it alongside her Billabong license. When Billabong began to take up too much of her time, she worked on Billabong exclusively. Cheron reflects Gordon's own obsessive interest and understanding in every aspect of the operation and has grown the SA market on the back of a string of successful events at Jeffreys Bay and vigorous sponsorship of the local surf scene.

NEW ZEALAND

John Snelling and husband and wife Mike and Lindley Court ran Billabong's NZ licence for many years – from the mid-'80s right up until the float of Billabong International in 2000. Mike and Lindley retired, while John stayed on as head of Billabong NZ for two more years then pased the reins over to Nilan Fonseka, an employee since 1990.

INDONESIA

Wayan Suwenda along with his wife Suzi was another surfer with a strong competitive background who moved into the surf industry with Billabong. Wayan not only guided the success of Billabong in Bali and Indonesia, but also helped John Innes get started in Singapore and Malaysia. He also makes sure visiting Billabong staff get their share of waves during Bali stopovers.

EUROPE

Europe proved a harder market to crack for Billabong. Two licensees failed before Gordon Merchant decided to place his trust in a young surfer from Victoria, Derek O'Neill, who'd been working for the previous licensee in the UK. Gordon's first move was to relocate the European operation to Hossegor, in south-west France, famous for its quality beachbreaks and idyllic surfing lifestyle. In typical style, the European operation had extremely humble beginnings. In the midst of a French winter, future CEO of Billabong International, Derek O'Neill, could be seen riding his pushbike to a small industrial shed on the outskirts of Hossegor. From here, Derek imported small quantities of Billabong product for distribution throughout Europe. He was soon joined by another travelling Australian surfer, Reid Pinder, shrewd enough to recognise a good business opportunity when he saw one.

Together, they helped grow the European market into the hugely successful business it is today. "I remember seeing Vince Lawder at the Billabong Australian Titles in 1986," recalls Derek. "He looked like he had the best job in the world. The surf industry in Europe was just starting up so I got myself there as fast as I could."

BILLABONG ACCESSORIES

Doug Spong and wife Mara along with his key henchmen Gary Nixon and Russell Norton took on Billabong's accessory program in the mid-'80s. New product lines in wetsuits, snow gear, backpacks and hats contributed greatly to increased revenue. "We'd never been a very good accessory company, " admits Gordon. "Doug's strength was always in product. It became a really good partnership, his products and our branding. That was part of a really major move forward with us." Billabong accessories are especially strong in Australia, where schoolkids carrying their books in Billabong backpacks is commonplace. "A lot of people in the Australian surf industry have got a lot to thank Doug for. A lot of his designs are still replicated," says Gordon.

BILLABONG GIRLS

The growth of girls surfwear has been one of the great success stories of Billabong's recent history. Reignited in 1992 in Australia by Rena Merchant and Heidi Bartholomew, the women's business has grown by as much as 100 percent in a single year, to the point where it now accounts for a third of Billabong's business. Now under the direction of Heidi in Australia, Billabong Girls has expanded into a global division within the group and continues to ride the wave of growth in women's surfing and fashion. In the USA, the girls line was only launched in 1999, with new management, and has enjoyed remarkable success in a short space of time under the design and direction of Cathy Paik and, more recently, Candy Harris' overall brand management.

BILLABONG TODAY

Billabong today is quite a different company from those early days at Gordon's kitchen table. The products can be found in 65 countries around the world. And the company, Billabong International, is a public company in Australia. All up, there are over 1000 employees that work under the same directions and guidelines that Gordon put in place over the years. "But Billabong's true strength comes from a huge group of passionate employees who live and breathe it 24 hours a day," says current CEO Derek O'Neill. "And Gordon gets to surf the most. That shows he got the balance right."

THE SINCE '73 CLUB

Despite such growth, Billabong remains deeply in touch with its roots. The Since '73 Club was formed to honour long-serving staff members. All staff with more than 15 years service were invited into the club, with 16 employees qualifying as foundation members. Heading the list is Patricia Taylor, who has been with Billabong for 28 years, most of that in the machine room until her recent move into merchandising. And a conscious policy of remaining close to its surfing roots, has meant that staff are still encouraged to take advantage of that most effective of de-stress strategies. It is no accident that the centres for Billabong's continued growth worldwide have emanated from many of Gordon's favourite wave destinations in Jeffreys Bay, Hawaii, the Gold Coast, Indonesia, south-west France and California. "One thing about Gordon is, no matter how hard he worked, he always maintained a policy of being close to good surf locations," says Dougall.

The famous left at Teahupo'o does not dissolve easily into the reef pass. Often, a righthander will mow through the peanut gallery, taking out any human or craft too slow to escape into deep water.

STEVE RYAN.

CONTESTS THAT CHANGED THE WORLD 〜〜〜〜 FROM KIRRA TO HONOLUA BAY TO TEAHUPO'O TO MUNDAKA, WAIMEA AND JEFFREYS BAY, BILLABONG

EVENTS CREATED A TEMPLATE FOR MODERN PROFESSIONAL SURFING. SUCCESSFUL CONTESTS RUN IN GOOD WAVES, IN EXOTIC LOCATIONS, AND AWAY FROM MAD SUNDAY SUMMER CROWDS........

kirra

90

What started as a $5000 contest co-sponsored with a night-club in 1992, grew into one of pro surfing's greatest showcase events. 1978 world champ Wayne "Rabbit" Bartholomew helped mastermind the humble, unrated pro-am over long afternoon chats about the state of world surfing with Billabong boss Gordon Merchant. A shared vision to stage surfing contests in quality waves led to the logical conclusion – a contest at Kirra, the world's most renowned righthand, sand-bottom, warm water, pointbreak barrel. Kirra had always been the yardstick by which surf fantasies were measured.

But the chances of scoring the fickle point were remote, to say the least, especially for a tight, weekend event. Over an entire cyclone season, Kirra might only break on half-a-dozen occasions. For Rabbit, searching for a new career direction after his lofty pro tour heights as event promoter and director, his beloved Point held his fate in its hands. On the days leading up to the event, anxious eyes watched the weather map. With exquisite timing, an obliging tropical cyclone spun into the swell window out in the Coral Sea. Obediently it tracked south until it hovered just east of the Gold Coast and pumped those ruled-edged ribs of swell onto the waiting, manicured contours of Kirra Point. Once was arsey, in the extreme. Twice, then three times in a row, was a ridiculous record the seemingly blessed union of Billabong, Bugs and Kirra barrels notched up. Munga won that first one, in a final packed with local talent. In a bold, communi-ty-minded experiment, free surfers were allowed to surf through the contest area, as long as they gave right of way to competitors. It worked brilliantly, and the locals gorged and the pro's rejoiced while the contest rolled in perfect four-foot tubes. "I remember Margo and Guy Walker, they'd never surfed Kirra. They were absolutely mind blown, that the myth was in front of their eyes and they were going to be surfing it in a heat," recalls Rabbit.

In '93, the desired cyclone almost came too close to the coast and the entire Gold Coast was closed out with whitewater to the horizon the day before the event. By the time the event started, it had settled down to a solid eight feet at Kirra, and an unstoppable Martin Potter won the title. Rabbit recalls the '94 event as his home break's finest moment. "I remember paddling out before the contest and (Tahitian pro surfer) Poto came by and said, this is the best surf he's ever seen in his life," says Rabbit. "That day it was, in my opinion, Kirra as good as it gets." Hawaii's Sunny Garcia won a sensational final but, more importantly, the fabled wave had helped fend off the threat of development. "There were talks of a marina at Kirra. We had a protest song at the time, Let Kirra Be Kirra, and at those contests,

Kirra spoke for itself," says Rabbit. "In '93 and '94 we had the best swells of the year and real-ly some of the best swells since. There was no room for waiting periods then. They were bulls-eyes." News of the epic event quickly spread and the contest continually attracted stellar fields of visiting pros, pumping waves and media coverage out of all proportion to its modest WQS ratings status. Not even a lacklustre year in '95 could dent its prestige, with the finals held at small Duranbah and won by WA's Jake Paterson. Inevitably, Billabong upgraded the Kirra Pro to full WCT standing in 1996.

Hawaii's Kaipo Jaquias won that first 'CT event, after a bold gamble by organisers to relocate to North Stradbroke Island for the semis and final. The event walked away from huge week-end crowds and mainstream media coverage at Burleigh Heads when the wind turned nor-east. A bus was hurriedly organised, and took the four semi-finalists and the whole contest entourage on the two-hour drive and ferry trip to the idyllic offshore island. Jaquias returned to his home in Kauai and promptly named his new-born daughter Kirra.

The '97 event enjoyed another classic swell at Kirra, highlighted by Shane Beschen's perfect heat, scoring three 10-point rides (a record still unmatched), a memorable showdown between a reborn Mark Occhilupo and world champ Kelly Slater, and a stunning victory for Slater. Burleigh turned on in '98 and the men's and women's events were completed non-stop in perfect barrels, over four-and-a-half days. Slater again took the coveted title. Beau Emerton won in '99 at Cabarita on the NSW Tweed Coast, as the event again went mobile chasing surf. And Sunny Garcia won his second title in 2000 at Duranbah.

The Billabong Pro was an event that helped define the art of mobile surfing contests at quality loca-tions with waiting periods – the tricky science of reading weather maps, making a call, strapping on the boards and going hunting for waves, with a bare bones contest infrastructure. When changes to the ASP rules forbade sponsors having more than three events on the WCT, and with contest com-mitments at Jeffreys Bay, Teahupo'o and Mundaka, Billabong had to reluctantly relinquish its treasured Kirra Pro. But the hard work had been done, and the so-called Dream Tour, with WCT events at a dozen or so of the world's greatest waves, was well-and-truly a reality.
– Tim Baker.

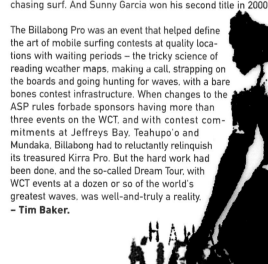

WINNERS

MEN

2000 Sunny Garcia [WCT]
1999 Beau Emerton [WCT]
1998 Kelly Slater [WCT]
1997 Kelly Slater [WCT]
1996 Kaipo Jaquias [WCT]
1995 Jake Paterson [WQS]
1994 Sunny Garcia [WQS]
1993 Martin Potter [WQS]
1992 Michael Barry [WQS]

Event winner Munga Barry with only the slightest of slouches and a feather-like touch during Billabong's 1992's debut contest at Kirra Point.
JOLI

Billabong PRO teahupo'o

TAHITI 2003

WINNERS

MEN
2003 Kelly Slater
2002 Andy Irons
2001 Cory Lopez

WOMEN
2003 Keala Kennelly
2002 Keala Kennelly
2001 Layne Beachley

teahupo'o

It seems almost kinda ludicrous to state this, but it's true: there's nowhere like Teahupo'o.
And that's why the Billabong Pro at this fateful location is absolutely essential to the sport of surfing. Teahupo'o is in fact the name of a small village at the end of a winding 60-kilometre road from Papeete, on the main island of Tahiti. The village – framed from the rear by the symmetrical jagged lava peaks made famous in a hundred surf mag line-up shots – faces the broad reef opening of Passe Hava'e. It's a short enough journey from the village rivermouth out to that wicked curve of coral; but each May for the Top 44 men and Top 15 women surfers on earth, it's the longest jetski ride of their lives. "You lie awake at night, tossing and turning," says Australia's Nathan Webster. "I do anyway... when it's 10 feet you can hear it roaring in the dark and you just think about the waves you might have to catch in the morning." Teahupo'o's freakish nature relies on two things: the dramatic step of the reef, jumping from depths

beyond 300 metres to near-dry in a distance you can cover with 30 seconds paddling; and the raw muscle of Southern Hemisphere winter storms, blowing swell from the Antarctic fringe thousands of nautical miles to the south-west. When the latter meets the former, something entirely unique in the world of waves is formed – not so much a wave as a curved ridge of water, a solid object that somehow moves. Match this against the ASP World Championship Tour, and you have the ultimate competitive moment. You can't run, you can't hide. It's a situation where a lifetime of effort is tested to its limit in just a few fearsome seconds. Tricks won't get you through this. Teahupo'o technique is about relaxation: being able to take the drop without tension, then draw smooth simple lines on a wave that constantly feels as if it's about to close out and drive you into the reef. It's more than talent: it's ingrained, which might explain why the same names surface over and over in the Billabong Pro final eight – winners Andy Irons, Kelly Slater, Cory Lopez and Mark Occhilupo, dangerboys Taj Burrow, Luke Egan, Mick Lowe and Kieren Perrow, and freak talents like Shane Dorian and Bruce Irons. The Billabong Pro Teahupo'o's Prime world tour ranking assures the winner of the highest possible WCT points reward. It's undoubtedly a critical rung in any surfer's world championship stepladder ascent. Yet what raises it above any other tour event is the esteem in which its winner is held. Not just by the wider surf community, who's been gazing slack-jawed at images of this superwave for almost a decade – but by the pro's themselves, who know just what the winner's had to put on the line. Like Mick Fanning says of Andy, for instance: "When he's at Teahupo'o, everyone knows he's going to turn and go, there's no question. It throws it back on you to do the same." **– Nick Carroll.**

jeffreys bay

"Dreams Are Free" it said on the front of the tee, and "Love Your Dog" on the back. It was the contestants' shirt for the 1991 Dream Sequence event at Supertubes, Jeffreys Bay. The Dream Sequence was an alternative format contest dreamed up in the sometimes obscure mind of Derek Hynd. What the phrases on the shirt meant no-one was really sure. When questioned DH said something along the lines that these were the two things that are steadfast in life, or something like that. Like death and taxes, we can be sure that dreams are for free, and we can be sure that if we love our dogs they'll love us back. Something else that is definite is that when the giant winter swells smash Cape Town between April and September and as cold front after freezing cold front batter the peninsula and wash giant ships aground, it'll only be a couple of overnight hours before perfectly groomed lines will be pouring down the mile-long righthander.

When Luke Egan won the Dream Sequence and a parcel of prime real estate on the point as first prize, he won it by smashing perfect waves over and over again with his powerful pivotal backhand style and driving turns off the top. In a similar vein and long before it was known as the Dream Sequence, an 18-year old Mark Occhilupo devastated big Supers on his way to winning the 1984 Country Feeling Classic, putting himself and Supers on the map. Through these years and today, South African licensee Cheron Kraak was responsible for the event's survival and success: First, as the Country Feeling Classic, then the Dream Sequence, the Billabong/Country Feeling and, now, its current title the Billabong Pro.

In its 17 years of existence, the Billabong Pro has had some amazing events. Included in it are a few Billabong Challenges and a continuous see-saw between WQS and WCT status. In 1999, 18-year-old wildcard Joel Parkinson became only the second wildcard in history to win a WCT event, the win signalling the arrival of a major new force in professional surfing.

In 1997, the remarkable Greville Mitchell and his Mitchell Surfing Foundation (MSF) provided the money to upgrade the contest to a WCT event, such was his belief in the importance of the event.

This importance is reflected in the event's winner's list. The wave is the ultimate test of a surfer's skill level and repertoire. The wave breaks fast and down the line and surfers need to string manoeuvres, thread a difficult, almond-shaped barrel and prove to the judges they can read a wave and link critical turns. It is a break of champions and there's no other wave that's a greater gauge of a surfer's style.

The town has grown, along with the event, from a small fishing village to a bustling tourist destination. It was also declared "the fastest-growing town in South Africa" a short few years ago. It is now an archetypal surf town with surfshops and clothing factories and shaping bays on every street corner. Apart from the screaming righthander at the northern end of town, the other things that holds this town together is Billabong's Cheron Kraak. From making boardies with her one sewing machine, Cheron has grown Billabong South Africa virtually by herself, and without wishing to detract from whomever the current mayor of J-Bay is, it's known and accepted by all that she's the lady of the town. This year, 2003, the fifth year in a row that the event held WCT status, Cheron was stoked. "It was great to see such good waves come this year as that enabled a lot more people to witness the standard of surfing that is being produced by the world's best surfers, which was absolutely incredible out at Supertubes on the final day," said Cheron. "It's also exciting to have the eyes of the surfing world focused on our town." That the event was won by Kelly Slater is secondary. He won it by surfing on a new level, and according to many critical eyes, surfed a few notches above the rest of the WCT contingent. The event was a cracker, with cooking surf for most of the time and local Billabong teamrider and wildcard giant-killer Sean Holmes using his local knowledge to take world champ Andy Irons out of the event for the second year running. Having no surfers in the prestigious WCT this year, it was a very proud and patriotic crowd who cheered Sean on as he blitzed his heat against AI.

Despite the event, the previous winners, the town, Cheron and all the local people, the real drawcard to J-Bay is Supertubes, the most consistently perfect righthander in Africa. **– Craig Jarvis.**

1. Dream Sequence mastermind Derek Hynd covers Luke Egan with a small piece of his contest prize – a prime piece of J-Bay land. 1991.

2. Cheron Kraak and Luke Egan.

3. Occy hacks at the J-Bay coal face. – ALL PHOTOS JOLI

4. 2003 poster.

Africa's jewel: long righthanders breaking at the perfect clip for the modern surfboard. (As viewed from the backyard of Cheron Kraak's beach house.)

BERNARD TESTEMALE

WINNERS

MEN
2003 Kelly Slater [WCT]
2002 Mick Fanning [WCT]
2001 Jake Paterson [WCT]
2000 Jake Paterson [WCT]
1999 Joel Parkinson [WCT]
1998 Michael Barry [WCT]
1997 Jevon Le Roux [WQS]
1996 Kelly Slater [WCT]
1996 Shane Thorne [WQS]
1995 Seth Hulley [WQS]
1994 Justin Strong [WQS]
1993 Michael Barry [WQS]
1992 No event
1991 Luke Egan [Dream Sequence]
1984 Mark Occhilupo [Country Feeling Classic]

WOMEN
2000 Megan Abubo
1999 Melanie Redman-Carr
1998 Trudy Todd
1997 No event
1996 Lisa Andersen

When the beaches of Hossegor reach 15 foot, good surfers make the two-hour run from France to the Basque town of Mundaka. Tide-affected, a rip that'll defeat any man, a difficult fast-running takeoff and fiercely-protective surfers make the Mundaka experience a true test of any surfer's skills. And thanks to Billabong Europe's Carl Wieser, whose communication and language skills ensure the event runs smoothly, the world's best surfers get to taste the unique and ancient Basque culture.

JOLI

WINNERS

MEN
2003 Kelly Slater (WCT)
2002 Andy Irons (WCT)
2001 No event
2000 Shane Dorian (WCT)
1999 Mark Occhilupo (WCT)
1990 Josh Palmateer (EPSA)
1989 Jeremy Byles (EPSA)

WOMEN
2002 Mens-only event
2001 No event
2000 Lisa Andersen
1999 Serena Brooke

1. 2003 contest poster.

2. Andy Irons, winner, world title year. 2002.

3. Occy, like Andy, used Mundaka as his leverage to world dominance. 1999.

4. Australian Jeremy Byles, pictured here and below, winner of Billabong's first Mundaka event, a contest that ran in waves of up to 15 foot. 1989. – ALL PHOTOS JOLI

mundaka

Only two triple-A surf spots on earth are overlooked by churches. One is Waimea Bay, on Oahu's North Shore. The other is Mundaka rivermouth. Quite apart from the symbolism – the silent seafarer's blessing implied by both buildings – there's an implied connection too. Waimea's birth as a surf spot brought a dramatic dignity to modern waveriding in its heartland, Hawaii. And Mundaka's growing legend has brought a similar classic-surf-spot dignity to the sport in a new heartland, Europe.

It's the perfect spot for the Billabong Pro, showcasing everything special about professional surfing, from North Atlantic power to the kind of deep-layered cultural roots anchoring WCT event locations worldwide.

The village of Mundaka sits on the western fringe of the Guernika River, about two hour's drive from Biarritz. Nominally, this is Spain; perhaps more accurately, it's Basque country – Euskadi, as it's known to the locals, a windblown coastal range of dark green river valleys and wooded mountain tops facing north into the Bay of Biscay. Autumn and winter, huge cold swells from storms off Ireland to the northwest roar in against the black cliffs and into the inlets, often ripped by powerful winds. Mundaka's fabled wave – on the right tide, with the right swell and the sandbar formed nicely by riverflow – takes this energy and forms it into a fierce sandsucking barrel, with a takeoff spot right in front of the Mundaka town harbour. Mundaka drags cries of "Kirra in reverse!" from the experienced traveller. But truth be told, a skilled surfer soon finds the rivermouth pit to be its own special challenge. Fresher than usual water means a thin board is a disadvantage; you'll sink just that fraction lower when paddling against the outward flowing current across the takeoff zone, and stall just that fraction sooner in a risky top turn. The wave bends in toward the sandbar and away to the other side of the rivermouth, creating deceptive tracks and angles and favouring a frontside approach.

In such conditions, an event like the Billabong Pro is thrown wide open – even heavier when you consider its critical role in the world championship race. Two-thirds of the way through the tour, this event comes at a turning point: a moment when bold champs-to-be can seize the ultimate upper hand and carry it unstoppably into the closing rounds. Of the past three Billabong Pro's, two have been won by surfers (Occy and Andy) who rolled on to the world crown. Then there's the church, a solid granite spire, backed by the stone village and its skinny streets, full at fiesta time with some of the happiest humans you'll ever meet. Basque culture can't help but flow into surfing. That passion, that dark-haired wild-country energy, with its original language and a history of living at least partly off the sea, seems naturally connected to Hawaiian culture and to the fundamental idea of something as energised and stoking as surfing.

And as in Hawaii, the Billabong Pro Mundaka relies for its success on local goodwill. The Mundaka surfing club, channelled by longtime ex-Aussie Mundaka resident Craig Sage, puts together all the pieces each day, knowing once the final's over and the winner's been given the traditional dunking in the harbour, they'll have their break back for the winter. **– Nick Carroll.**

hawaii

In 1984, pro surfing in Hawaii was shot to pieces. The Billabong Pro Hawaii changed all that. Beginning in 1985's winter as a tentative new beginning for international ASP-style competition on the North Shore of Oahu, Gordon Merchant's visionary event grew into a benchmark for an era when pro surfing was growing faster than it knew how to handle.

No other event dared quite as much: first, in opening doors for new kinds of surf contests in an arena where pro surfing's advancement had been halted; second, in offering the kind of money that'd take over a decade to become standard practice at the elite pro level.

First a bit of history, if you can stand it: When the Association of Surfing Professionals was first launched at the end of 1982, it began a political war between Hawaii's pro events – and their creator and promoter, Fred Hemmings – and the rest of the pro surfing world. The ASP's fore-runner, IPS, was Fred's baby, and neither Fred nor ASP head Ian Cairns were noted for their gentle diplomacy. The upshot: in 1983, Fred's events, the World Cup and Pipeline Masters, were declared out-of-bounds for the top pros. The following year, the World Cup made a minor comeback as a B-grade ASP event. It was something; but to astute observers of hardcore surfing like Gordon, leaving Hawaii out of the picture was a major limit on professional surfing's credibility.

So was born the Billabong Pro, a contest designed to re-create some of the original power behind great old-school North Shore events like the Smirnoff Pro and the Duke Classic. As with the Smirnoff, the Billabong was declared mobile between Sunset Beach and Waimea Bay. The move paid off immediately, with '85's winter producing big sloppy waves suitable only for the Bay, and for the winner: graceful four-time world champion Mark Richards.

Then came 1986. Oh my God, 1986. Sorry, a bit more scene setting. It's hard to imagine in these days of 50-foot tow-ins and general huge wave mayhem; but back in the mid-1980s, big-wave surfing was way off the surfing mainstream map. Almost every ASP event was held in surf under four feet. It came as quite a shock, then, when the 1986 Billabong Pro's opening day was greeted with a full-on 20-to-25-foot north-west groundswell. The first real set of the day arrived about halfway through the second heat. It turned the horizon black and sent the four surfers – MR, Ross Clarke-Jones, Rob Bain and Almir Salazar – scampering out to sea, not to catch the damn thing but to avoid it. Richards and RCJ managed this; Bain and Salazar were smashed and had to swim in, after receiving directions from lifeguard Darrick Doerner.

During the course of that classic day, each competitor had to make choices he'd never expected to make. Some charged and were honourably flogged, like Rabbit Bartholomew and Martin Potter, who

dug rails on the way down the face and found out that, yes, wiping out at Waimea was every bit as bad as you'd imagine. Two – Bryce Ellis and Gary Green – chose not to surf at all, figuring (probably sensibly) they just weren't up to the task, and thus set a precedent that's never been deliberately met again by any pro, anywhere. And just a few charged and pulled it off with serious style: California's Richard Schmidt; RCJ, whose big wave career was set on its merry way; and MR, who flowed through a situation he'd first faced 12 years before as a 17-year-old Smirnoff Pro rookie, and who a day later at Sunset ended up winning the whole thing.

Big-time competition in Hawaii was back in the limelight, and a chain of events was set in motion that would ultimately lead to the Prime-loca-tion structure of today's WCT. But the Billabong Pro Hawaii was far from done. In 1987 it played a starring role in Gary Elkerton's sensational double victories at Sunset Beach. In 1988, ticketed to go fully mobile along the North Shore, it provided the stage for one of the greatest world championship showdowns in surfing history. Several surfers, including Tom Carroll, Damien Hardman and Barton Lynch, had shots at the title, and when the Billabong Pro's final day dawned on perfect 10-foot Pipeline, it seemed as if Carroll's day had dawned too. But the 1987 Pipe Master fell to a priority interference, and Lynch surfed a nerveless, incredible four heats to win the event and the crown.

For 1989, after that amazing Pipeline day, Gordon sensed something special was required. Digging deeper into the marketing budget than anyone else had yet dared, he sent prizemoney spiralling to a total of $US225,000, with $US50,000 for the winner and the biggest ratings points pool ever. Needless to say this sent most of the pros into a minor frenzy. But motive, not frenzy, wins big surf contests, and no surfer had more motive – financial and ratings and performance all included – than Cheyne Horan. The pro veteran, on the verge of dropping off tour and freshly ignored by his old-time sponsors, turned everything around in perfect eight-foot Sunset Beach to edge out none other than 1986 hero Ross Clarke-Jones and bank the cheque and the career-saving points.

In 1990, the event provided the great American world champion Tom Curren with the final step in his epochal third world-title run. On a wind-blown, wet Sunset day, Curren picked up a second in his early round heat, came in, and hugged his mentor, surfboard designer Al Merrick. The Curren legend was complete. Young Aussie Nicky Wood took the major prize in sloppy medium-sized Sunset. It was good stuff, but Gordon and his team knew the best of this event was already in the past, and they decided to let go while they were ahead. Pro surfing was on the brink of another change, one that wouldn't fully find its form until the Billabong Super Challenges and other perfect surf events of the mid-1990s. In the meantime, the Billabong Pro Hawaii had served its purpose with pride. **– Nick Carroll.**

1. Deceptively benign 20-foot Waimea Bay.

2. Four-time world champ MR came out of retirement to win back-to-back Billabong Pro's in '85 and '86.

3. Artwork for the most cashed-up surfing event in history, the winner enjoying a $US50,000 payday.

4. Californian Richard Schmidt surfed brilliantly at big Waimea, taking off on top-to-bottom 20-footers. — ALL PHOTOS COURTESY SURFING MAGAZINE

WINNERS

1990 Nicky Wood [WCT]
1989 Cheyne Horan [WCT]
1988 Barton Lynch [WCT]
1987 Gary Elkerton [WCT]
1986 Mark Richards [WCT]
1985 Mark Richards [WCT]

Mark Richards, a four-time winner of the world professional surfing title, and a legend well before the Billabong Pro events in Hawaii, emerged from retirement to take back-to-back wins in giant surf at Sunset and Waimea. Confirmation, as if it was necessary, of a Great Man's continuing brilliance.

WARREN BOLSTER.

The objective of The Super Challenge was to test a rejuvenated Mark Occhilupo against the world's hottest contemporary surfers, including world champion Kelly Slater, prior to any tour return. In the years after his premature retirement from pro surfing, Occ had drifted away from the sport he loved, had gained weight and was lost in a seemingly hopeless spiral. Determined to get Occ back into "fighting shape", Jack McCoy and Gordon Merchant created an invitation-only event at a remote reef in Western Australia. Occy proved he was more than competitive... proved he was a genuine threat... and qualified the year after for the grand prix WCT tour. Three years after that, in 1999, Occ was crowned world champion. Kelly Slater, a close friend and occasional heavy rival of Occ, squeezing into one of those perfectly foiled Western Australian desert tubes.

TED GRAMBEAU

THE ☒ SUPER CHALLENGE

MOTIVATED BY A DESIRE TO TEST A RECHARGED MARK OCCHILUPO → AGAINST A PACK OF TOP PROFESSIONALS JACK McCOY HELPED CREATE THE SUPER CHALLENGE –I– AN ANNUAL INVITATION–ONLY EVENT SET IN ISOLATED LOCALES FROM WESTERN AUSTRALIA TO SUMBAWA. IT WAS A CONCEPT THAT WOULD CHANGE PRO SURFING FOREVER.

BY SAM GEORGE

Images from The Desert Super Challenges, events that brought together the hottest surfers in the world to duel against the New Occ. (This photo, then clockwise): Occy, the star of the whole deal, warms himself against the cold Western Australian desert night; 1995 winner Rob Machado; a four-way draw in 1996, from left: Luke Egan, Rob Machado, Occ and Kalani Robb; Fresh Indian Ocean lines pour onto the north-west's most challenging reef.

ALL PHOTOS TED GRAMBEAU

I got my first look at surfing's future through the zippered front door of a tent. It was 1996 and I was camping on the coast of Western Australia where the blasted umber desert of the Sunburned Country is torn from south to north like a strip of paper, revealing a crystal blue sea beneath. My tent site on the station perched itself over the Indian Ocean, the view a neatly-layered parfait of parched earth, turquoise water and even bluer sky.

In the distance, long, even swells rolled down the reef, thick, powerful waves exploding and winding down the line like some kind of horizontal tornado. Absolutely going off. If I closed my eyes the images played themselves out against my lowered lids. Occy, Machado, Potter, Egan, Robb and Paul Paterson, Williams and Dorian. The way they rode that wave was… it had to be seen to be believed. Which was precisely the point. And it was why I was here in the desert, along with eight of the world's best surfers, for a very special sort of competitive surfing event. An innovative and ultimately progressive format based on a simple premise: take the world's hottest surfers, cut them loose in the world's best waves and may the day's best man win. No reeking circus tents, no sordid bikini parades, blaring loud-speakers or soggy, blown-out Sunday afternoon final. Instead, clear, bright, defined surfing performance.

Sure, there were coloured jerseys. And yes, there were judges who would eventually determine a winner. But the vision behind this new groove asserted that the real winner would be the bigger, broader surfing world, treated to a competitive format that ennobled a surfer, rather than turning him into a dancing bear. That vision was The Billabong Challenge, the inspirational surf "contest" that changed the face of competitive surfing forever. Promo hyperbole? Surf journo bullshit? Well, consider this. Before the first Billabong Challenge in 1995, there were no WCT professional events held at Grajagan, Tavarua, Tahiti or Mundaka. No Mentawai Islands boat trip specialty events, no super-group September Sessions videos. The idea of a select group of top surfers expressing themselves competitively in perfect waves at a remote location was still in the realm of fantasy. And yet in the wake of the series of Billabong Challenges that were held between 1995 and 1999, the entire format of world championship professional surfing morphed from its post-'70s, bad waves-and-bunting sensibilities, into an international circuit on which the best surfers are put in the best waves at the best times of year and encouraged to go off. A year-long, global Billabong Challenge, if you will.

Appropriately, the concept was born at one of the international surf world's most magical spots. "We were in Indonesia in the early 1970s," remembers renowned cinematographer and Billabong Challenge co-founder Jack McCoy. "And I'm sitting there at Uluwatu one day, and we had just been into Kuta to watch the Ali-Frazier fight on some restaurant's TV set. Remember, this was in the early days of professional surfing, and after watching the big fight I'm sitting there at Ulu thinking, 'I want to get Wayne Lynch and Gerry Lopez out here to Uluwatu and have a surf contest.' A real soulful little thing with two of the best surfers in the world in a really beautiful place, in great waves. All inspired by the Ali-Frazier fight – that's what planted the seed for The Billabong Challenge."

Fast-forward 20 years or so. The still soulful McCoy has become the surfing world's greatest filmmaker and father of the modern surf video. Having produced a number of innovative videos for Gordon Merchant's Billabong company, McCoy has also become a close friend and adviser to surf phenom Mark Occhilupo, the former world title contender who by the early '90s had experienced a serious career melt-down. With a combination of emotional and financial support Merchant and McCoy were instrumental in orchestrating Occy's comeback. But by 1995 something special was needed to prove that Occy truly had got his surf chops back. "Basically, Gordon and I were thinking about how to get Occy back in fighting shape," recalls McCoy, with a chuckle. "We decided to run a little contest, and figured we'd invite Tom Carroll, Martin Potter and Tom Curren, all of whom were off the ASP tour at the time, and see how Occy measured up. But when one of the surfers became unavailable, we thought, 'Why not invite the four top ASP surfers?'"

By the time of the last Billabong Challenge in 1999, Occ was in his world title year and dominating a tour he first joined in 1984. Mark Occhilupo, swooping through the bowl, Big Rights.

JASON CHILDS

The surfers, the photographers, the journalists, the family that evolved from five years of classic surfing contests.

Three Hawaiian surfers, all pivotal members of the Billabong team at some point in their careers: Sunny Garcia (driving), Shane Dorian (still with Billys) and Kalani Robb.

JASON CHILDS

The idea of some sort of specialty event already appealed to Merchant, who at this point had been under a lot of pressure from the ASP to underwrite conventional events. But the Billabong founder, a former shaper and still an accomplished surfer himself, found his interest steering in alternative directions. McCoy, in the meantime, was already there. "We really wanted to establish something we felt would be positive for surfing," says McCoy. "You've got to remember that at the time most big pro contests were held at city beaches with the finals at two pm on a Sunday afternoon, regardless of surf conditions. Well, Gordon didn't want to do it that way, didn't want to invest his money in that. It was time for something new."

That something new was the first Billabong Challenge, to be staged at a remote location in the Western Australian desert described as The Mystery Left. True to McCoy's early vision, it would consist of a handful of top surfers – Kelly Slater, Rob Machado, Shane Powell, Sunny Garcia, Johnny Boy Gomes and Occy – who would camp on this isolated sheep station's shore and wait for the best of the best swell during the two-week waiting period. No bleachers or contest scaffolding necessary. Only the sheep drovers and a few of the indigenous Yamaji Aboriginal tribe would be on hand. The event would be filmed from just about every angle, though, and produced by McCoy for a video release.

Great concept. But pulling off the first Challenge was still a... challenge. Remembers McCoy: "My wife Kelly, her sister Tracy and husband George Simpson° and I organised and ran the whole thing, from the film crew to the camp site. The toughest thing was getting everybody in the right place at the right time. The location we had chosen is very remote – it's hard enough just getting there on a surf trip, let alone the sort of trip we had in mind." The sort of trip McCoy and Crew had in mind didn't initially sit well with the region's, let's say, "protective" local surfers, none of whom were overly enthusiastic about having some pro surfing circus set down on their idyllic surf zone. But then they'd never heard of an event quite like The Challenge, whose organiser was quick to explain wasn't your typical surf contest. "The initial resistance came from people who didn't understand what The Challenge was trying to do," explains McCoy. "Once we had an opportunity to sit down and talk with them, explaining what we wanted to do and impressing on them that we'd really do everything we could to remain true to the sprit of the event and its location, everything opened up. And we have been true. We never once mentioned the name of the break where we held the first two Challenges. It was just The Mystery Left. In fact, even though nowadays everyone knows where it was, the name still hasn't come out of my mouth. Not on film, not now. So I've kept my word."

McCoy kept his word to the pro surfers too. From the first moment contest director Wayne "Rabbit" Bartholomew stood up on the hood of a nearby ute and waved his red jacket to start the event, it was all about the surfing. McCoy had assembled a knowledgeable panel of judges, including George Simpson, a rugged outback surfer and one of the wave's pioneers, Wayne Murphy, another top West Oz

continued page 108

Western Australian Paul "Antman" Paterson joined the Desert Challenges as a cook but ended up competing in both when invitees didn't make it – first, Luke Egan in 1995, then Kelly Slater the year after. Jack McCoy remembers his powerful surfing in waves Ant'd been surfing since he was a kid, and his sharp humour. When asked by the camera-wielding McCoy for a quote before he paddled out, he replied: "I've got Occy, Kelly, Powelly… just a light heat." Here we find Antman, late, committed, and driving down a rapidly concaving face despite the Indian Ocean about to land on his shoulders.

TED GRAMBEAU

Ten feet of pure east swell flicked the switches of the South Coast's reefs prompting surprise, as well as a nervous anticipation, among competitors.

JASON CHILDS

Kelly Slater took out The Challenge in South Africa at 10-to-12-foot Jeffreys Bay. With his magic on the rail like this, his stand-up barrels through Supertubes and his perfect timing paddling out through the difficult impact zone, Slater pocketed $US20,000.

LANCE SLABBERT

Hawaiians Sunny Garcia (back) and Shane Dorian.

JASON CHILDS

Hawaiian Kalani Robb, a regular at the Billabong Challenge, captured mid-tube during 1999's South Coast Challenge.

JASON CHILDS

goofyfooter, and renowned surfer/shaper Maurice Cole, who had first accompanied McCoy to this stretch of desert during the filming of Stormriders back in 1982. Creativity was encouraged, as each surfer was expected, even within the competitive structure, to surf exactly as he pleased, without the normal constraints of 20-minute heats and blown-out beachbreaks. In the end, Rob Machado came away with the victory, but everyone involved knew they had participated in something special. "Rob and Kelly, especially, were really inspired," says McCoy. "They went back to the rest of the ASP, going 'We just did something amazing. We just had an incredible experience.' And so we had no trouble from that point getting people involved."

Technically, there were four more Billabong Challenges: another held at the isolated station, then at Jeffreys Bay, Sumbawa and the South Coast of New South Wales. Each had its classic moments, its memorable surfing, its standout surfers. Not all were held to completion; not all produced individual winners. On a number of occasions the surf conditions didn't warrant the competition, so, keeping true to its original mission statement, The Challenge surfers actually split the prizemoney rather than compromise the event's creative integrity. But in many ways, individual winners weren't what The Billabong Challenge was all about in the first place.

Sunny Garcia and The Turn of 1999's Challenge, a bold piece of surfing on a wave that created uncertainty in all but the most experienced big-wave surfers.
JASON CHILDS

DOING IT FOR THE KIDS

BEFORE THEY ASSUMED THE ROLE OF TODAY'S HIGH — PROFILE SURFSTARS ✫✫✫ TEENAGERS WERE BLOODED IN THE LAWS, TACTICS AND PRESSURES OF PRO SURFING VIA THE  BILLABONG ✗ ➡ ➡ JUNIOR SERIES

BY JJ

Six months before he became the world junior champ, 18-year-old Joel Parkinson became only the second wildcard in history to win a WCT event, the 1999 Billabong Pro at Jeffreys Bay. "When they created that series, they created us," says Joel of the Billabong Junior Series. "It made us who we are."

ROB GRIFFITHS

Joel Parkinson, star graduate from the Billabong Junior Series.

TWIGGY

(This page)... just another hot young kid, Shane Felsinger, feeling the joy of a good bottom turn at a warm-water point.

SIMON WILLIAMS

(Far right): Shaun Cansdell, one of the hottest teenage surfers in the world – air-reverse shot on Super 8 film for the movie Because I Wanna.

CHRIS SEARL

"WHEN THEY CREATED THAT SERIES THEY CREATED US, IT MADE US WHO WE ARE." Joel Parkinson, 2002 world number two.

"AS A CONTEST MODEL, I WAS ALWAYS KIND OF WONDERING WHY THE REST OF THE WORLD DIDN'T EMBRACE IT. JUST SEEING HOW WELL IT WORKED AS A GROUNDING AND A GROOMING TO BE A PROFESSIONAL SURFER, IT WAS JUST THE BEST PLATFORM ONE COULD IMAGINE." Rabbit Bartholomew, President – ASP International, 1978 world champion.

The numbers speak for themselves. In an era where more than half of the current Association of Surfing Professionals (ASP) Top 44 elite are Aussies, every single surfer has competed on, or contributed to the Billabong Junior Series. Five others, including two American world champions have competed and triumphed in the internationally-recognised Billabong Junior Challenge events and World Junior competitions. That's one helluva legacy.

How'd the Junior Series begin? Go back to 1991. To a wind-blasted carpark overlooking Margaret River in Western Australia. Tim Duff, a local surf contest director, was engaged in passionate conversation with then Billabong team manager, Vince Lawder, who was planning a major tournament on Oz's western shores. "I remember it clearly," recalls Vince. "It was a freezing cold day, really windy, and we were standing on the bluff overlooking Margaret River where the Masters is traditionally held, and Tim said, 'God, open men's surfing is stale. There's a gap to be filled, you should do something with the juniors, they're unpredictable, they're exciting.' And he was right. Little did he know, we were actually planning to do a full circuit." The first tent pegs where driven into the sand a few months later at Duranbah, a consistent beachbreak on the New South Wales/Queensland border. A second event took place shortly after on the urban fringes of Sydney at Cronulla."The demand that first year was huge," recalls Vince. "It was immediate, there were hundreds of entrants, like we'd uncovered oil. It just exploded. We knew right away we were onto something, that there was no turning back."

While its illustrious namesake, the Pro Junior at North Narrabeen, had been crowning future world-beaters since 1977 via its single-event status, with the emergence of a full-blown domestic circuit, heroes, personalities and reputations sprouted virtually overnight. More importantly, however, was the release of this competitive animal in Australia's adolescents. Nathan Webster, Richie Lovett, Jake Paterson, the Bannister brothers, Shane Wehner, Shane Bevan, Sasha Stocker, Grant and Jason Frost, Dylan Longbottom, Dan Wills, Jye Gofton, Paul Ward and Michael Lowe are but a few of the names who cut their teeth in those early days, fighting watery duels along

Australia's foreshores, and in the process, elevating the junior performance bar to new heights.

Surf magazines at the time ran stories espousing the virtues of such new talents, with headlines like: Who will beat Slater?, The 'New' New School and The Doop Generation. Hot 100 polls became an annual event and talent scouts were forced to turn one eye south from the lofty heights of the ASP's glitzy international circus and confusing qualifying series, to the Next Big Things, not so quietly tearing apart their local beaches and reefs. "I remember it as a very special time," says Mark Occhilupo. "The way Billabong structured the events was perfect. For me, especially, because as one of Billabong's older surfers all we had to do was show up and surf the expression sessions which they had at every event. I was in a pretty reclusive state at the time, I was just coming out of my retirement so to be able to be in that environment, at all those amazing places with the kids surfing amazingly. I mean what a good way for me to come out of that period, you know? It got me inspired."

Fittingly, the venues for such events were as glamorous and varied as the individuals who participated in them. By the mid '90s, events were being held in prime locations like the Gold Coast, Rottnest Island, WA, and the remote desert outpost of South Australia's Yorke Peninsula. "We established this great formula to the point where we'd show up at a particular spot and the local crew would be like, 'Unreal, they're back!'," explains Lawder. "We'd have our dates planned out, itineraries and check-lists were drawn up for the mums, dads and kids – really pointing out everything they'd need for a particular place, especially spots like Yorkes which were in the middle of nowhere. We'd do promotions with local surf stores and radio with our top level surfers, then hold the contest and expressions sessions and just have a really great time. The kids learned to respect the land too. Occasionally you'd see one of them chuck a can or smash a bottle, and the other kids would pick them up on it. Like, 'You bloody idiot! Whaddya thinkin'!?'. They'd totally write each other off, then make them clean it up. So much money is poured into keeping the land in its natural state. I think travelling taught them that, taught them respect."

If there's one thing that deems a surfing competition a success – above the most conscientious of planning or the weight of its prize-money swag – it is waves. Within its 12-year history, the Billabong Juniors Series has enjoyed conditions unparalleled by any circuit outside the ASP's restructured formula-one Dream Tour. Much credit is given to the vision founder Gordon Merchant and his team has had on revamping major competition via the selection of unique world-class venues and the introduction of extended competition windows, or 'waiting periods'. The success of concepts such as The

Billabong Challenge projects – the invitation only made-for-video, freeform competitions held in the best available waves – which have been based on this criteria are legendary. And just as the ASP has benefitted from this model, it's no coincidence that the Junior Series has also.

Even so, current ASP president Wayne "Rabbit" Bartholomew is stunned at the amazing luck he and Lawder shared as co-contest directors. "Phenomenal is the best way I can describe it," says Rabbit. "We were catching places on the day of the year, and it was one after the other. Just amazing. We'd arrive at these places and the locals would be going 'Aw, it's pretty crap,' then we'd wake up at first light, go down to the beach, and it'd be six foot and offshore and we'd look at it and go, 'Well, it must be another Billabong Junior event'. We'd run right through to the finals, the last hooter would blow and then, from out of nowhere, the onshore would appear... Is there an explanation for that? You tell me."

Given such circumstances, the performance levels continued to climb through the roof. Even the women's division, which in surfing, rightly or wrongly, is so often considered an adjunct to the main show, excelled. In 1997, when the raw Indian Ocean peaks of Strickland Bay on Rottnest Island topped eight feet, causing a buzz of excitement and anticipation in the men's camp, the female competitors shocked all when they insisted they too be allowed to surf. "It was unheard of," remembers Lawder. "I mean there were triple-overhead waves breaking that day, and Strickland's is a really heavy set-up."

Prior to the event WA contest official, Tim Thirsk, buoyed by the enthusiasm of his own daughter, had reluctantly agreed to include the division. Staring out at the wild sea, however, and at another freak Billabong swell, he began to regret his decision. "Tim was just going, 'Nah, Vinnie, it's not going to work, mate'. But I'll never forget it, everyone said the chicks grew balls that day. They went out there and went off." Local West Australian Holly Monkman. Byron Bay's Jenny Boggis, Celia Miller and eventual '97 Series winner Stacey Emerton, competed in the final. When they returned to the beach having tamed the giant peaks, the men promptly stood and applauded. "I guess we really felt like we had something to prove, especially with all the best guys watching," recalls Monkman. "I remember wanting to win so bad I actually rode my last wave right onto the reef. It was so shallow and I just got smashed. I had all these cuts on my knees and blood was dripping everywhere. When the heat finished, guys actually ran down to the water and clapped the girls as we walked back up the stairs to the cliff. I know the next year when they had the event again in Western Australia, it was big then too and the girls went out and did the exact same thing."

As the increase in performance levels endured and reputations continued to balloon, international recognition followed. Teenagers from destinations as far flung as South Africa, Great Britain, South America and Florida began arriving in Australia specifically to compete in the Series. To Merchant, who by now had enjoyed incredible success with his two Challenge events, it became obvious that the next logical step was to emulate the concept, but using juniors. So that same year, eight surfers were chosen, flown in, and as the cameras rolled they surfed it out along Australia's East Coast for a $US20,000 first-place cheque. The magazines lapped it up. Jack McCoy's team again captured the colour and magic Billabong's ventures were becoming synonymous with and the futuristic manoeuvres the grommets performed were so spectacular, the resulting film was eventually named after one of them, Alley Oop. "I just remember at the time it was one of the most amazing events for a junior to be in," says Taj Burrow, one of the original Junior Challenge invitees. "With the guys in it, I just figured it was the best way to see who was doing the new tricks and who was inventing new airs and stuff. I mean we had Andy (current ASP World Champion, Andy Irons), Chris Ward, Sean Holmes, CJ (eventual 2001 ASP World Champion, CJ Hobgood), Tim Curran, Mick Lowe… you look at where all those guys are now, it's crazy."

The Challenge's overall format couldn't have been any simpler – inventive, free flowing and improvisational, just like the grommets themselves and exactly the way Billabong figured it should be. "Besides a camera in your face every now and then," says Burrow, "we'd just surf, eat and do our thing all day. Outside of that it was all about trying to beat each other. It was ON and everyone loved it." Although Californian Tim Curran (ironically, the pioneer of the alley oop manoeuvre) would go on to win, a passionate rivalry was sparked between both Burrow and Irons. Laughing, Irons recalls how McCoy was forced to discipline him during his first serious trips to Oz at an age where he was still "very rough around the edges. We were groms going for it, so Jack talked to me a couple times, mellowed me out. But it was an exciting time, for sure. We all became good friends right away and I think there's still some stuff which never made the film, you could say some of it was R-rated."

The following year a second Junior Challenge was held. Called Wide Open, the difference from the previous event was overseas competitors now had to fight for inclusion through localised qualifying trials. Continuing its evolution, Merchant saw the potential for the Junior Series to go international. At the time, Graham Stapelberg, the Executive Director of the ASP, had put together a global proposal to integrate a junior qualifying series and junior world championships as part of a third tier to the ASP world tour. Gordon immediately agreed to underwrite the end of year junior world championship

event for three years, which was now supported by a fully-fledged qualifying tour in each of the ASP-designated regions to select the top juniors from around the world. Today, there are strong junior qualifying series in Australia, USA, Hawaii, Japan, Brazil, Europe and South Africa. Billabong is proud to sponsor over seventy percent of all the regional qualifying junior pro events that take place around the world.

And so, for the first time, surfing crowned its own junior world champion in 1998. "That was when it was brought forward to the ASP," says Bartholomew. "And I mean, what an evolution. The Billabong World Junior Championship was, and still is, a completely individual title. I went and co-contest directed the first one in 1998 with Craig Inouye at Mailee Point in Hawaii and it was such a brand new thing, it was fantastic. Of course history shows Andy won, and when you look at any of the surfers who have achieved the same, they've all gone on to be the best in the world." Andy says he keeps his inaugural World Junior trophy atop his TV set at his home on Kauai, and whenever he looks at it he's reminded of what he regards as the start of his competitive career. Now, at 25 years of age and with a second men's world title well within his grasp, he "trips out" at the memories and rivalries he still enjoys with the top-ranked surfers who have all graduated from the same meritorious order. "You look at Parko (Joel Parkinson), I mean he won the World Junior twice and we've already competed in two finals together this year," says Irons. "And last year we were one and two in the world, so that's pretty wild, pretty cool how it turned out like that. It's like I still see his ugly mug every day! Then there's Taj, CJ, Rasta (David Rastovich)… all those guys were there. It was the best stepping stone I could have hoped for, for sure."

Parkinson, the Series' most dominant performer, is emphatic in his praise for it: "I don't even think Billabong knew when they started the Junior Series that it could be so good, I don't think they even realised how much they were doing for Australian surfing at the time. Now, when we surf at top level competition, we're still doing the same stuff, using the same strategies, using everything we learned back then… it was intense, the most intense friggen competitions ever. For me back then, it was everything."

These days, as its graduates take up spots on the main stage, the World Junior has re-established itself on Australian sands, at the original hotbed of east coast surfing dominance, North Narrabeen. Now the junior world championships will become even more significant as it will provide the top two finishers with the opportunity to secure increasingly important seeding qualifications into the round of 96 in all four-to-six star WQS events for the following year. This concept was initiated by Billabong Europe's Reid Pinder and rounds

out an efficient and defined career path for future pro surfers.

From a modest beginning at Duranbah, Billabong has created a structured path and paved the way for the future stars of surfing.

BILLABONG JUNIOR CHALLENGE CHAMPIONS
1997 Tim Curran, California, USA.
1998 Taj Burrow, Yallingup, Western Australia.

BILLABONG WORLD JUNIOR CHAMPIONS
1998 Andy Irons, Hawaii, USA
1999 Joel Parkinson, QLD, Australia.
2000 Pedro Henrique, Saquarema, Brazil.
2001 Joel Parkinson, QLD, Australia.
2002 (no event)

Ace Buchan, a talented young Australian who developed his competitive skills in the Billabong Junior Series.

TODD MESSICK

115

SURFING AND THE GIRLS

A LOVE STORY

****

THE RISE AND RISE AND RISE AND RISE OF GIRLS ON BOARDS

BY KAI STEARNS

Keala Kennelly's taken to the world's heaviest lefts like no other girl, which has encouraged other girls to follow suit. "As I kid, I was made feel like I was moving in guy territory. Now girls think, 'Hey, I can do that'." Pipeline, North Shore winter, 2002/03.

VINCE CAVATAIO

Keala Kennelly's snarling. She peels herself off her board and to her feet like you'd separate two parts of a surf decal. Her arms rise to ten and two to absorb the inevitable push from landing late at the bottom of a wave that, without exception, rattles everyone who surfs it. Teahupo'o. All but unsurfed 10 years ago, now an annual stop on the men's and women's pro tour. Guy surfers fear and revere it in all the right ways. Keala's there. She's not crazy... but she surfs it like she means it. Even that, for girls, tells a story that demands respect.

Beneath the smiles of modern girl surfing is a history of women scratching for cred in an ocean of moving goalposts. From Margo Oberg's charging of Sunset in the '70s to eventual four-time world champ Frieda Zamba to Jodie Cooper, Pam Burridge and Wendy Botha's professionalism, the girls were paying double dues for half the respect. "They'd compete because they wanted to," says Keala. "Those girls would win and still lose money." It was frustrating, but already it was clear to these girls that surfing had something to offer, changing them in ways it didn't do for the guys. To these girls, surfing was a different gift.

But the big change that moved girls and surfing toward the centre came in the late '90s and started miles from the beach, in a book called Girl Power: Young Women Speak Out. In it, author Hillary Carlip redefined the way the world looked at teenage girls. These girls were smart, savvy, troubled, and pissed-off. They talked about their real lives — sex, gangs, family, rape, disorders, friendship — and it wasn't all pretty. But the point was that from the book and the Girl Power movement that followed, girls became emboldened, empowered, and a community unto themselves. For the, the focus wasn't just on boys anymore – the catching of, the competition with — and in that shift, the groundwork for change was laid.

Here was a notion that poured directly into the heart of surfing. Guys had felt it for years and, whether through apathy or some weird form of selfishness, had kept it to themselves. But now women had discovered the giddy, adrenalised effects of surfing. Riding waves tore at the mental constraints of daily life even while it made you fit and beautiful, hyper-aware and superhuman. Surfing brought to these girls precisely what the guys were trying to keep from them: Power. Still, it took a while for the significance of these

Layne, comfortable in Fiji.
PAUL NAUDE

Keala, late but solid at Teahupo'o.
SCOTT NEEDHAM/SNP 5000.COM

changes to dawn on the surfing industry, mostly through the talents of one woman in particular. "It has a lot to do with Lisa (Andersen)," says five-time world champion Layne Beachley. "You really can't put it any other way. She made it alright to be a girl. She was feminine and beautiful and she absolutely ripped. Those things weren't mutually exclusive anymore."

While your average guy will claim not to care, girls didn't have to pretend. They could have it all. And while guys might buy one pair of boardshorts a year, girls weren't afraid to have a little more fun with it and buy a swimsuit and a few pairs of shorts to surf in, a suit to tan in, and whatever else that took their fancy. For all the commercial realities this represented, the overwhelming truth was girls were ready – eager, even – to redefine the surfing lifestyle as it related to them. In less and less subtle ways, surfing was changing forever.

The '90s belonged to Lisa and Layne. Two good-looking, media-smart, talented surfers who finally accomplished something of a holy grail – making women's surfing attractive and accessible to everyone. These were the crossover success stories that women's surfing needed to cement itself into the main-stream's consciousness.

They were aided by appealing marketing campaigns and the rise of women's surfing magazines. In 1995, Wahine in the USA became the first magazine created especially for girls who surfed. It was followed in 1998 by Chick in Australia and Surfing Girl in the US. Having spent the last 40 years as barely a sidenote in men's surfing magazines, the women finally had a substantial place to make their own headlines and showcase their skills. Girls who lived nowhere near the beach could now begin to understand and appreciate the surfing lifestyle. And they did – in droves. With all of these pieces in place, girls and surfing were in for the long haul. The time was ripe for a classic surfing authority to join the game.

119

Stand-alone events mean better waves for the girls. Layne burns speed at Honolua Bay.

TOSTEE/ASPWORLDTOUR.COM

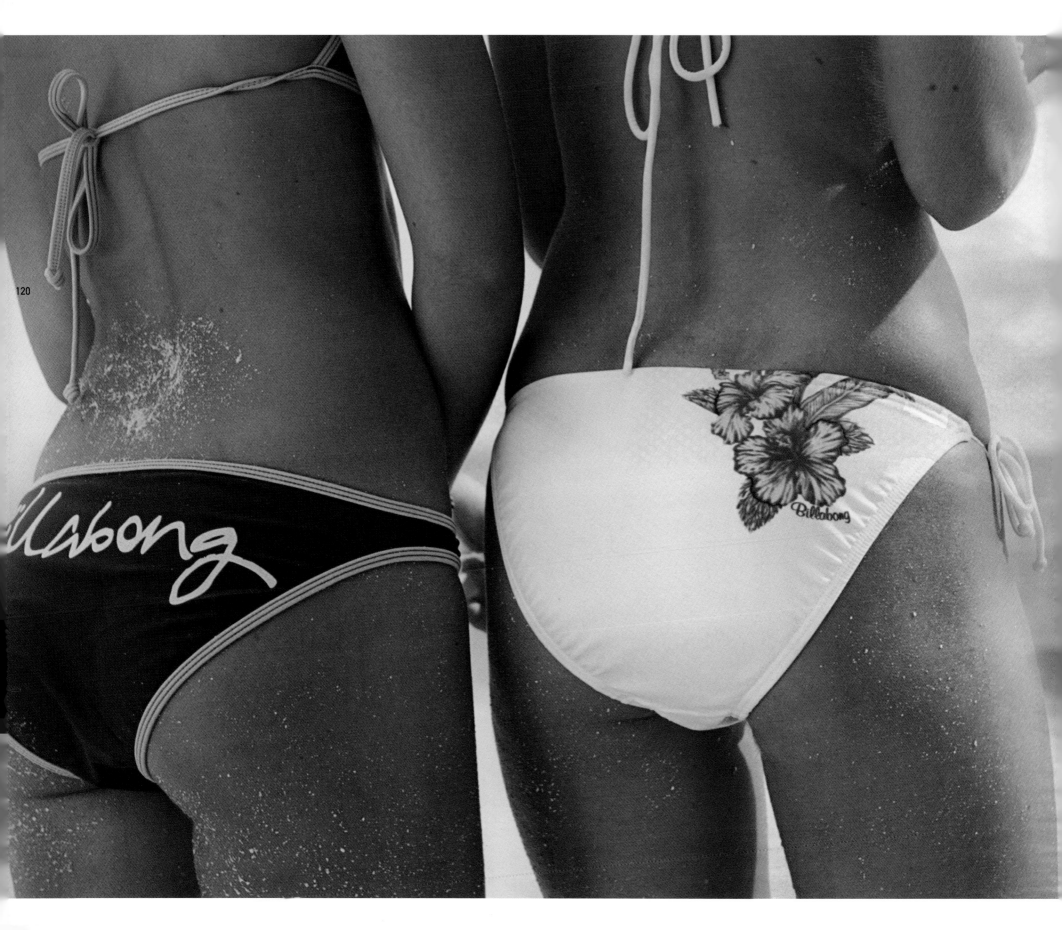

"The boardshort phenomena set the pace," says Billabong Australia's Heidi Bartholomew, who worked closely with Rena Merchant in developing the girls division. "Girls got their own, stronger identity. It was the sexiest thing, girls wearing boardshorts meant for their bodies. And surfing is such a cool and sexy thing to do. We gave the girls empowerment, helped them feel good about themselves."

The team roster is a great indicator of how successful a surf company is, and like the formidable men's line-up, the Billabong Girls' team speaks for itself. World champ Beachley is the figure-head, backing her contest victories with a resume that includes riding the world's biggest waves ever by a female. And then there's Keala: an idol for girls willing to give the middle finger to conven-tion. It's a yin-yang combo that works.

Back in the early days, a shortage of quality events and a lack of prizemoney meant going pro was hardly a viable career path. Women were often sent out in the worst conditions of the day – in order to save the best waves for the guys – and the cash for winning was routinely a tenth of what the men were paid. As late as 1993, former world champ Pauline Menczer had to work side jobs just to get the money needed to travel to the contests.

All of that changed when big companies like Billabong Girls began to host world-class contests at classic spots, upping the cash purse in the process. Billabong sponsor two of the most incredible spots on the tour, with the Billabong Pro at Teahupo'o, and a women's stand-alone WCT event in the long rights of Honolua Bay in Maui. Stand-alone contests like Maui are crucial because they allow the girls to be the main draw and focus. That, and Rochelle Ballard's work forming the girl's own administrative body (the IWS), brought the women's tour closer in parity with the men, if only in that they had a chance to surf the same waves.

...continued page 124

Boardshorts might have made them famous, but bikinis were in the mix even back when Billabong kicked off 30 years ago.

SCOTT NEEDHAM/SNP5000.COM

1. Sanoe Lake surfed long before Blue Crush made her a Hollywood celeb.
— SCOTT NEEDHAM/SNP5000.COM

2. For years, girls couldn't even get a decent pair of shorts to surf in. It's a subtle but fundamental shift. — SCOTT NEEDHAM/SNP5000.COM

3. All speed and rail, Layne burns past the camera in Tahiti. — SCOTT NEEDHAM/SNP5000.COM

4. Kate Bosworth heads out to Pipe.

5. Despite the clichéd Hollywood poster, Blue Crush took the surf industry by surprise when it traded the classic macho stereotypes for an authentic look at a rookie's struggle on the North Shore.(From left): Michelle Rodriguez, Kate Bosworth and Sanoe Lake.

6. While the lead actresses learned to surf and even paddled out at Pipe, some things take a lifetime to learn. Rochelle Ballard goes where the celebs couldn't.

Billabong understood the need to put the idols among the fans as often as possible if they wanted to keep the momentum going. The Get Out There program and Billabong Boarding School are initiatives in Australia and the USA designed to teach girls of all ages how to surf in a fun, safe and encouraging environment. Team riders give pointers and sign autographs. there's plenty of freebies flowing and tunes from an on-the-beach DJ bring as many girls as possible to the party.

Perhaps Billabong's most influential contribution came from its involvement with Hollywood movie Blue Crush. Industry insiders were justifiably wary of another Hollywood shot at explaining surfing. But not only was Blue Crush a hit, it turned out to be the most accurate portrayal of the surfing lifestyle since John Milius' epic Big Wednesday.

It's staggering how far women's surfing has come in the last 10 years. "As a kid, I was made to feel like I was moving in on guy territory", says Keala. "Mags never made me feel like I was included. Now the mags make girls think, 'Hey, I could do that.'"

"The biggest change is the younger girls are bargained over and fought for," says Layne. "It never happened when I was a kid. Now girls are poached. Companies realise the value of good girls on their team."

Of course. there's always more to accomplish, but now there's momentum instead of inertia. Girls learning to surf now enjoy a world where women pro surfers are respected and financially solvent. It's a new age when women in the water are no longer a freak occurrence. And the world's line-ups are better for it. "Surfing makes you feel good about yourself," explains Keala. "That's the secret. That's stoke. And the best part is that girls get that feeling now." 🏄

(From left:) Liz Cantor, Rebecca Woods, Layne Beachley, Alana Brennan and Keala Kennelly. Tahiti.

Kiana and the classic South Pacific ensemble.

For men or women, the fundamental pleasures remain the same. Sanoe Lake and Alana Brennan in a Tahitian duckdive.

ALL PHOTOS SCOTT NEEDHAM/SNP5000.COM

THE ⊜ ODYSSEY

✗ ✗ ✗ ✗ ✗ ✗ ✗ ✗ ✗

↳ A SELECT GROUP OF HIGH-PERFORMANCE SURFERS JOIN A HOMERIC THREE-YEAR SEARCH TO FIND, AND RIDE, A 100-FOOT WAVE: AND TO MAKE IT REAL INTERESTING BILLABONG KICKS IN ||| $US 500,000 ||| TO THE MAN WHO CONQUERS IT ⬅

BY EVAN SLATER

The scale of tow surfing has moved from beyond awesome to the truly surreal. Mike Parsons rides a 66-foot wave at the Cortes Bank, one of the biggest waves ever successfully surfed. "A flush comes over you afterwards," says Mike. "When you're out there it's super noisy, like being on a tarmac next to a 747 – there's this huge rumbling, roaring and shaking. But riding, you don't hear a thing."

ROB BROWN

128 **We felt so small out there, watching history speed past our "purist" souls.** Lost in the channel, 100 miles off the coast of San Diego, captain John Walla and I could only scream like little girls as Brad Gerlach snapped Mike Parsons into his now world-famous "66-footer" at the underwater shoal known as Cortes Bank. Fifteen minutes before Parsons' life-changer, we were young Roger Ericksons, sitting proudly on the peak on our 9'8"s, confident we'd catch a few the old-fashioned way. But we had never seen open-ocean swells move as fast as this (35 knots, according to forecast expert Sean Collins), and had lost the battle before we even jumped off the side of the Pacific Quest. By the time the second set loomed on us, we were done. Walla barely escaped a trip over the falls by punching through the lip and – after paddling for and missing the first one – I had the pleasure of turning around and watching a 40-footer jack up and pitch 20 yards in front of me. It was this little episode that prompted us to shamelessly drop anchor in the channel and submit to the New Big-Wave Order. "I guess this is Tow-ville," admitted Walla.

Good thing we had come to that conclusion so soon. If we hadn't, we probably wouldn't be here to tell you what Parsons' wave looked like. It was significantly bigger than any other wave that day, and Snips just happened to be in the slot for his very first ride. He was already S-turning when it was still a huge, shapeless lump, but when it started jacking over the mountain range 20 feet below the surface, he prepared for some serious rappelling. One quick fade, and the rail-thin Snips on a skinny 7'2" tow board became a small, black speck on the face of El Capitan. Taking a traditional big-wave line, Parsons sat in the trough of the massive wall for a split-second before giving his 16-inch-wide water ski everything he had to make it around the next thundering section. "I think he got weeded!" yelled Walla. But Parsons stayed planted and kicked out 100 yards inside to the disbelieving cheers of everyone who witnessed the one-wave freak set. To all eyes at sea level, Parsons' January 19, 2001 feat represented the epic conclusion to the big-wave space race. After all, no one will ever match such a giant ride with such a shocking discovery in the middle of the ocean… right?

Well… maybe not. To other visionaries on the scene, Parsons' wave proved that anything is possible with a PWC. Three hundred feet above us, in a twin-engine Cessna, Project Neptune architects Larry "Flame" Moore and Bill Sharp could hardly keep their lenses focused. They'd been dreaming of a successful Cortes mission for the past 11 years, and now that the day finally arrived, Sharp couldn't help but think this was only the beginning. The former Surfing magazine editor and Katin CEO had already made a Maverick's-size impact with his K2 Big-Wave Challenge in '98 and the XXL Big-Wave

While some moan that surfing's greatest spots have already been discovered, The Odyssey reloads the entire discovery process. Like laying a codebreaker over the pages of a book, at over 50 feet, old spots change character while brand new spots reveal themselves. One of the newer discoveries, Cyclops, off the southern Australian coast.

TED GRAMBEAU

130 Awards in 2001. Essentially photo contests (the shot of someone riding the tallest wave wins), these two big-money events generated more international buzz than any world title race. Sharp knew how to push buttons in both the surf world and the mainstream media, and Cortes proved to be the inspiration for arguably the greatest endeavour the surf world has ever seen. "Just looking down from the plane and seeing it all play out made me realise that there had to be thousands of Cortes Banks out there," remembers Sharp. "And I wanted to create something that would allow us to find them."

Initially called Project Sea Monster, Sharp ordered the world's bathymetric maps and started marking the potential hot spots. At the same time, he looked for a way to frame his mission as a marketable event. The frame quickly found its backing when Sharp met with Graham Stapelberg and Paul Naude of Billabong USA. Wanting to expand its presence in the big-wave arena, Billabong signed on Parsons and challenged Sharp to come up with a viable project they could embrace.

By the summer of 2001, that project – The Billabong Odyssey – grew to titanic proportions before it even left the docks. The hook? Over a three-year period, the world's best tow surfers would pass up the obvious big-wave haunts and roam the high seas in search of the 100-foot wave. And they wouldn't do it just for fun. The surfer who rode the biggest wave at the end of each year would be awarded a cash prize of $US1000 per foot of the wave's estimated face height (for all you maths flunkees, Parsons' 66-foot Cortes bomb would've netted him $US66,000). In addition, the surfer who rode the biggest wave of the entire Odyssey would be awarded a minimum of $US250,000 and, if the wave exceeded the 100-foot mark, it would go as high as $US500,000.

It had adventure. It had big stakes. And it had one, round number that everyone could understand: the Sasquatch-like 100-foot wave. "I think everyone involved is willing to turn their backs on the sure bets for the next few years and really see how far we can push it," said Sharp at the time. "I mean, does the surf world really need another big Mavericks session?"

Today, more than two years into the Billabong Odyssey without a 100-foot scalp on the mantle, Sharp realises his claim may have been a little premature. He also realises the Odyssey, like any voyage, evolves according to the whims of the ocean. All of his initial objectives are still viable: a handful of the world's best tow surfers are still seeking out the largest surf on the planet. But what he's come to realise is that the Odyssey surfers are much more than a renegade gang of big-wave bounty hunters. They're model citizens of the ever-expanding tow world, passing on knowledge, safety procedures and inspiration to the small bands of power surfers on every continent. Dozens of sessions, several new spots and count-less giant waves after Sharp dreamed up the concept, the Odyssey is leaving permanent impressions on the big-wave world that will never get lost in the channel.

IMPRESSION ONE: SAFETY FIRST
"We're taking this very seriously – it's incredibly important that we build a base layer around safety." Billabong's Graham Stapelberg made this clear from the start: the Billabong Odyssey isn't about a bunch of daredevils tempting fate – it's about a group of well-trained, well-prepared "risk technicians" who know how to deal with any heavy situation the ocean spins their way.

So, before the 2001 winter season revved up, Sharp and Team Odyssey purchased six Yamaha 1200 cc two-strokes, a whole mess of gear and headed to the mouth of the Columbia River along the Washington/Oregon border, better known as the "Graveyard of the Pacific." There, they joined up with the Cape Disappointment Coast Guard and let the ultimate authority on water safety, Makaha's Brian Keaulana and his team, give them a crash course on PWC mas-tery and life-saving techniques. First on the curriculum: five hours in the classroom. It wasn't much different from a high school history class, except that guys like Darryl "Flea" Virostko, Ken Bradshaw, Shawn "Barney" Barron,

You could say Layne Beachley's driven – rather than towed – into big waves. No other woman has dedicated as much time to the chase. Western Australia.

TED GRAMBEAU

132

Vetea David has been the face and spirit of Tahitian surfing for the past 15 years. Always a performer in heavy waves and a powerhouse on the pro tour. Poto shifted his energies to the emerging tow scene and instantly felt at home. Teahupo'o.

JON FRANK

Keaulana didn't make it easy on them. He introduced terms like Safety Risk Management, Random Hazard Identification and Incident Command Systems and bombarded them with enough acronyms (A.C.E., S.S.A.F.E., P.C.-S.E.L.F.) to confuse even the most dedicated teacher's pet. Still, the message at the end of it all was crystal clear: know your surroundings, be prepared, have a system in place with your group and, according to Keaulana, "deal with the mouse, not the monster." The real test came at the end of the five-day training course, when Keaulana sent the teams out into 40-mile-an-hour winds, pissing rain and endless rows of storm surf along a 28-mile stretch of Washington beach. The task? Retrieve your drowning partner, who's really a Chinese tourist clutching onto a family heirloom. "It was classic," said Ken "Skindog" Collins about his rescue attempt. "Barney was just spazzing out, going Jackie Chan on me. He was fighting me the whole time." Aside from a slippery Keaulana who kept getting away from Parsons, the surfers passed tow-in boot camp without any casualties. And even more important than all the newly-acquired skills, the crew left with perhaps the most important preparation for the big-wave unknown: trust in each other.

It's this trust that allowed Gerlach to find Parsons in giant French beachbreak surf later that winter after a communications failure separated them for 10 minutes. It kept Gerr and Snips' heads together when they were lost in the fog coming home from a giant day at Todos. And it gave Shane Dorian the tools he needed to make the proper rescues when his partner, Noah Johnson, went down during 2002's super session at Jaws. As Dorian said at the end of his Pacific Northwest re-education camp, "I came here just to learn about the equipment, but I learned way more than I thought was even possible."

IMPRESSION TWO: A SKI IN EVERY PORT

"The elusive 100-foot wave? It was right here. And no one was here to ride it." Six weeks after The Billabong Odyssey training camp in the Pacific north-west, it was almost as if Maverick's – along with the spot's spokesman, Jeff Clark – heard Sharp calling it out. A complex low formed in the Aleutians, sending a super-charged, early season swell topping the Oregon buoys at 42 feet at 20 seconds. The only problem was, Sharp's proposed spot at the mouth of the Columbia River had about 50 knots of south wind on it. No go for The Odyssey.

Meanwhile, Mav's saw arguably its biggest day in recorded history with sketchy but rideable conditions. Brazil's Carlos Burle, Clark and the Santa Cruz crew had the rides of their lives before a storm front set in, but after the last tow team called it quits, water patrol Shawn Alladio swore she gunned it over a 100-foot set. Experts like Grant Washburn and Jeff Clark later verified her claim. It wasn't what Sharp wanted to hear, especially since The Odyssey's lack of options forced him to merely survey the ragged but historic swell as it rolled on down the coast. "There was a real learning curve at the beginning," says Sharp. "Expanding the knowledge of the ocean, really understanding the probabilities of getting surf at these out-of-the-way places. And what quickly became obvious was that there just isn't enough of a window for spots like Columbia River – you can't get there fast enough. You really only get four or five shots of huge waves each winter, and it's tough to roll the dice on those. After November 21, we adjusted our mission statement."

The new mission statement went something like this: The Billabong Odyssey wouldn't just be in the middle of nowhere; it'd be everywhere. Every time the forecast charts went purple, Sharp would be on the phone, organising skis and crews and support teams. In a sense, the Oregon-trained Odyssey members were now more like tow-in SWAT teams, ready to perform heroics whenever and wherever things got heated.

The new quick-response squads got The Billabong Odyssey moving in the winter of '01/'02. It put Layne Beachley in the spot for her benchmark 20-foot-plus wave at Todos. The big-wave chase made Gerlach and Parsons miss Thanksgiving, Christmas and New Year's and put them in harm's way during some midsummer mega-swells at Teahupo'o. And, most noteworthy, it helped spark one of the greatest big-wave sessions ever in November. '02, when The Odyssey split peaks with Maui's strapped crew on a 50-foot-plus day at Jaws. "It was the most amazing day I've ever seen," says Sharp. "The rapidity at which the level had risen in two years was just unfathomable. Dozens of guys rode waves over 50 feet. And they weren't just surviving them; they were ripping them." Billabong made another wise adjustment in the winter of '02, incorporating Sharp's original XXL Awards concept into an offshoot of the Odyssey. Not only did the surf world's chief big-wave expeditionary force operate under the Billabong banner, but now the company attached its name to the largest wave of the winter, wherever it might land. Called the Billabong XXL, it doles out $US1000 per foot to the rider of the year's biggest wave. Eighteen-year-old Makua Rothman won the inaugural '02/'03 event for his 66-footer during the Jaws session, proving once again that you can never turn your back on the big-wave staple spots.

IMPRESSION THREE: LEAVING TRACKS

"Next year, we will win. There is no limit to this reef." Frenchman Sebastian St. Jean said this at this year's Billabong XXL, after his last-minute entry from Belharra (a mysto break two-and-a-half miles off the coast of St. Jean De Luz) nearly turned the surfing world upside-down. The mammoth left tied Makua Rothman's wave for the biggest wave of the winter, but since St. Jean was further over on the shoulder, Rothman won. But to even entertain the idea that a wave in France – or Chile or West Oz or Ireland, for that matter – measures up to Jaws would have been unfathomable a couple of years ago. And, for the most part, the surfers in these areas admitted as much, not even bothering with the hunt.

But with The Billabong Odyssey and the Billabong XXL as incentive, this is changing. Parsons, Gerr, Skindog and Virostko were in France in early '02, checking Belharra and hanging out with the French tow surfers, including St. Jean, Fred Basse and Peyo Lizarazu. The swell was too small or a session, but the

cultural exchange planted the seed the Frenchman needed for when the Day of Days did finally bloom. A similar thing happened during The Odyssey's recent adventure to northern Chile. The giant left outside their main break has always thundered with few – if any – takers. But after witnessing what Dorian, Parsons, Adam Replogle and Brenden Margieson were doing on their tiny tow boards, local rippers like Ramon Navarro and "Flecha" now have upgraded equipment and are ready to follow the same path. "We left our skis down there and passed the torch on to those guys," says Sharp. "They'll be on it when it's big." Over time, The Billabong Odyssey is likely to have "sweeper cells" like these at every spot with big-wave potential. Margieson is heading up the mainland Oz/Tasmania/New Zealand task force, and they're looking to establish "branch offices" in Capetown and Ireland.

IMPRESSION FOUR: OUT THERE

"We're carrying 4/3s, booties, gloves, hoods, ropes, extra ropes, gas cans, a compass. It's four in the morning, pitch black, and Gerr and I are motoring out to some new spot together. It just feels so cool, like we're the only people on earth. I look around sometimes and go, 'What's everybody else in the world doing right now?' We just feel so alive out there." Two years ago, when Mike Parsons signed on as The Odyssey's main protagonist, he did it for one primary reason: the feeling. Not for the cash, the fame or even the chicks (the dude's 38 already). No, he did it for the feeling he gets when it's him and his partner, teetering on the edge of the world, surfing some terrifying new spot. It's the feeling he had during his virgin Cortes session in 2001, the feeling he'll try to recreate as long as his body – and The Billabong Odyssey – allows him. Despite all of The Odyssey's adjustments, this ideal remains at the project's core. Sure, they've broken new

Hawaiian royalty, Makua Rothman, winner of the Billabong/XXL and $US66,000 for this wave. Jaws, November 2002.

TOM SERVAIS

ground in two regions instead of 10, but those two adventures – south-west Australia and northern Chile – remain Parsons' fondest Billabong Odyssey memories. "Chile was the first time we were completely prepared for a wave," says Parsons. "It was this big, fast wall of a left and the guys were just ripping it. Dorian was flying on a 4'11" and Brad was doing these giant carves, saluting a Jesus statue on the cliff as he raced down the line. It was like we all discovered a new level in tow-in performance surfing. South-west Oz, on the other hand, was just hardcore," says Mike. "First, we covered this series of islands by plane, using a map to mark all the spots with potential. Then our guide Bernie, who came equipped with four skis, a double-decker trailer and an arsenal of gadgets, drove us 50 miles off the nearest paved road and in search of the best launch spots. We had to find ways to hoist skis down cliffs. It was crazy. "The first spot we surfed was like giant Winki Pop. Super high-performance, about 10-to-12 feet and just me and Ken Bradshaw. Nothing scary, but it still got your blood pumping since it was new territory. Plus, there were giant whales camped out in a nearby bay. I'll never forget it. Then there was the spot we're calling Cyclops. This was later in the trip, when a local ab diver showed us around on a boat. He told us of the wave, but he said he didn't think it was rideable. When we pulled up and saw these thick, right mutants shelfing beyond belief, he was half-right. Layne [Beachley] was like, 'You guys are stupid, don't even think about it.' Ken was like, 'That's not my kind of wave.' So Brad and I watched it for a while, assessing it, using some of those risk management techniques Brian taught us. If we did eat it on this wave, we were eight hours from a car and however long from a hospital. Some waves went completely dry on the shelf; others were kind of makeable. Then we saw this incredible set that was wide enough and deep enough and I'm all, 'We're out there.' Those kind of ledgy reef waves are hard to tow because you can't track the swell very far, but we did get a few. Actually, the best wave I caught was the first wave I went on. How exciting it was to ride that wave and then try to figure out what boards would have worked better. It's what The Odyssey is really all about. I remember watching waves out there, completely frozen and in awe of what the ocean was doing. To know that those kind of waves are still out there keeps me going."

It's also what will keep The Odyssey going. Whether you're on the sidelines or in the thick of it, the mysteries of the deep are tough to ignore, especially when guys like Parsons are so close to solving them. How deep will The Billabong Odyssey take us over the coming years? Strangely enough, Parsons is sure they'll end up right back where their voyage started. "We have a better understanding now for how all the big swells work in the different oceans," he said. "And you know what? You just can't help but think the biggest wave – that 100-footer we all talk about – will be at Cortes."

It may not surprise Europeans who've known and surfed big waves off their Atlantic coast for a generation, but for the rest of the world this inconceivably large wave at St Jean de Luz near Biarritz seriously blew minds. Sebastian St. Jean pictured here on a wave no human could ever paddle onto.

CHRISTOPHE DIMULLE

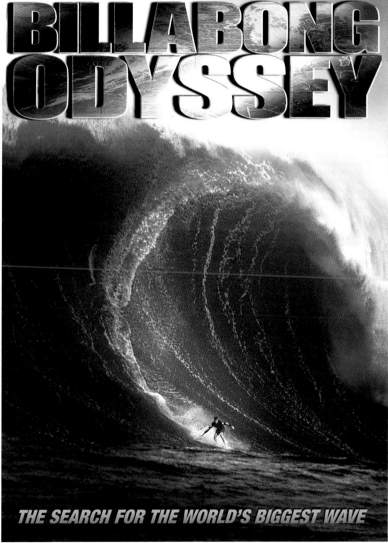

BILLABONG ODYSSEY

THE SEARCH FOR THE WORLD'S BIGGEST WAVE

EAT, SLEEP, SURF 〰
AND WATCH → SURF VIDEOS
━━ ━━ ━━ ━━ ━━ ━━ ━━ ━━ ━━ ━━ ━━ ━━ ━━ ━━
━━ ━━ ━━ ━━ ━━ ━━ ━━ ━━ ━━ ━━ ━━ ━━ ━━ ━━

IN 1987 HUMANITY WAS SUFFERING
HEINOUS CORPORATE POP,
JEANS HOIKED TO NAVELS AND

BY JAMIE BRISICK

THE BIGGEST STOCKMARKET CRASH
SINCE THE DEPRESSION. MEANWHILE
THANKS TO A NEW MEDIUM,
PERFORMANCE SURFING
WAS QUIETLY GIANT ✕ ✕ ✕
TAKING A GIANT LEAP.

Andy Irons, the star (with Rasta) of Jack McCoy's latest opus, Blue Horizon, 137
at a wave he co-owns with his brother Bruce and a handful of Tahitians.
SCOTT AICHNER

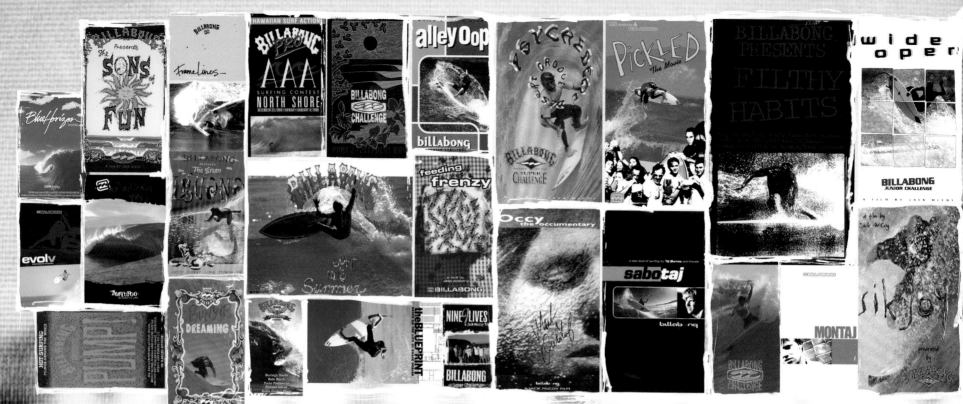

From 1987's Surf Into Summer to 2004's Blue Horizon, Billabong movies provide snapshots of performance surfing in each epoch.

Aside from the birth of the thruster in the early '80s, nothing has done more to lift the performance bar than videos. In fact, if you track surfing's timeline, you'll find that the curve remains fairly flat through the first half of the century – board design was advancing and wave riding was evolving, but there was no real medium to spread the latest and hottest surfing. This changed radically in the early '60s with the birth of the surf film. Surf films did more than just sell-out theatres and stoke up the kids – they were a vehicle that showed what the best in the game were doing. If you surfed in solitude at some off-the-beaten track place in the country, you could at least tap in to a surf film to see what was happening at Malibu or Makaha, a couple of performance hotbeds in the '60s. The performance curve sharpened upward with the arrival of the Surf Film, and became even sharper with the birth of video in the mid-'70s. No longer did you have to wait for the movie to hit your local theatre, now you could hit Rewind/Play, Rewind/Play, Rewind/Play in the comfort of your own home. And you did more than just watch 'em... you studied them. This was a huge breakthrough. Never before had high-performance surfing been dissected so thoroughly. Billabong released Surf Into Summer in 1987, a time when videos were to surfers what porn mags are to prison inmates. Occy, Matt Branson, Jason Buttonshaw, and Rabbit give a glorious taste of what can be done with a long reeling righthander and Surf Into Summer video marks the beginning of a revolution. Since then, Billabong has been responsible for a thick catalogue of classics that have caused more than one remote control to be rubbed raw. Here are a few highlights:

PUMP

Pump picks up where Surf Into Summer leaves off, only we're now in 1990, the beginning of a new decade and a new movement. Tail slides are a big part of the package and Occy, Richie Collins, Munga Barry and the late Ronnie Burns go nutso – inspiring kids the world over to lift their game and turn up the volume.

SIK JOY, BUNYIP DREAMING and THE GREEN IGUANA

Aside from all the sick surfing, there's a moment in the Green Iguana that's not to be forgotten – Occy's alter ego Rocky, despite brother Margo's warnings, decides to leave his life as a fisherman and go off and find world-class waves. He gets them – in WA, in Indo, in Hawaii – and his surfing looks a helluva lot like brother Occy's. In fact it is, which is why, on an imagination level, TGI is brilliant.

The real story goes like this: Filmmaker Jack McCoy had been shooting a long-haired Occy going whacko for a few months. Then there was some off time. In that off time Occy got a short haircut. When he showed up to shoot the rest of the film, McCoy flipped. Continuity – something that filmmakers think about constantly – was lost. As far as editing the film goes, it would be a big kink in the flow. After pondering ways to get around this, McCoy (with writer Calli Cerami and artist Graeme Davey) came out with Rocky. Rocky rock 'n rolled. Rocky was a new-and-improved, shorter-haired Occy, an Occ alter-ego that was electrifying. McCoy managed to add comic relief at a time when the video market was saturated with tons of high-action but minimal imagination. The trio of Sik Joy, Bunyip Dreaming and The Green Iguana are hallmarks by McCoy. The shots are luminous. The TV screen glows in ways that make you want to drench yourself in saltwater and smack the lip seven or eight times in the process. The soundtracks cause you to twitch and tap toes. These are more than just surf videos: they're injections of stoke served up in greens, blues and graphic hallucinations. McCoy's memories of the movies are classic. On Margo, who made his debut in the Green Iguana, he recalls: "I was shooting an early funky Billy Kirra contest. The waves were small, it ended up in The Iguana. And in there too you will see a long tuberide of Margo's. The waves were good and Munga, Luke, and Occ were going off. And Margo... well, the first couple of waves I saw him on I was blown away. I really dug his style and his ability. After shooting that long tube seen in the Iguana, I yelled up to Bugs who was in the shed and said 'Who is that guy?' 'Margo,' he answered. I cracked up. But he made an impression on me. A couple of days later Gordon signed him. I'd never met the guy, but based on those couple of waves I was prepared to back him. Even with a name like Margo.

"About a month later Occ and I were in the north-west when Shane Bevan had to go home and I needed another surfer. Luke and Munga had gone back on tour and they sent me Margo. Occ and I picked him up at the little country airport that was two hours from where we were staying and this shy gangly kid was there, blown away that his hero was meeting him. He made it clear from the start that he didn't want to be called Margo. Anyway, with all his shyness and sincere doodle-doop-de-doop, I began thinking, what the hell have I done here? I started to have all of these doubts about the kid and wondered what Gordon would say if I'd made a bad call here. All of that was washed away when we arrived back at the spot with a vicious, shallow, sometimes exposed, bubble in the middle of the reeling left. I still remember sitting on the hill with Stu, the local caretaker and extremely hot surfer, watching Margo paddle into his first-ever wave at this spot – it was a solid eight foot – flying down the line heading to the critical dry reef spot, and Stu saying 'Let's see how he handles this?' What he did then I'll never forget. Instead of going high and avoiding anything to do with the mess, he went straight up, hit the lip vertical, make that past vertical, landed it and kept going, making the wave. Stu and I looked at each other in disbelief. 'I've never seen anyone ever do that there,' he yelled, and he'd seen lots of hotties through there from Carroll to Banks, but a backsider of all people. I smiled to myself and knew my job was secure. It took me about two weeks to convince him that his nickname could be one of his greatest assets. We even played up the fact when the film came out about a year later with the 'Don't call me Margo' line. It stuck. And to this day I'm probably his biggest fan. All around legend in my book."

THE BILLABONG CHALLENGE PARTS 1 & 2, PSYCHEDELIC DESERT GROOVE and NINE LIVES

Take nine of the best surfers in the world, load 'em up in a car and travel south of Sydney, seek out the best possible waves within a respectable waiting period, hold a contest, and film the whole process – from the carpark moments to the heaviest cuties to a bloody cantankerous, raging righthander that not all wanted to be a part of, to the handshakes and hugs at the glorious end. Nine Lives is part surf contest, part anthropological study. It's reality TV before reality TV became a thing. Most of all, it showed once again that if you pick out the right venues and wait for the right days, a surf contest can be all about great waves, as in the case of the big Sunset Beach-like spot that Shane Dorian and Sunny Garcia revel in. With Rob Machado, Kalani Robb, Shane Dorian, Luke Egan, Tom Curren, Sunny Garcia, Taylor Knox, Pancho Sullivan and Occy as leading men, and Jack McCoy as auteur as well as contest organiser, Nine Lives won the 2000 Surfer magazine "Video of the Year" award for best cinematography.

Of the Desert Challenges, Jack remembers a turbulent time with Hawaiian Sunny Garcia, something that made for great footage: "When it came to the Desert Challenge, he was having problems at home and clearly did not want to be there. Gordon told him he had to so there was not a lot of co-operation from him. I was in charge and he took it out on me. I just kept the cameras rolling. He kinda played it up for the movie. This was a film that I'd set my objective to get into the different personalities and, for me, Sunny could pout all he wanted. I knew it made for a good story. As Sunny drove away in his rent-a-car for the last time, we didn't need to add any sound effects as the car had been thrashed by his daily two-hour, high-speed drives over the dirt road both ways. After the movie's release a lot of people told me how sorry they were for me and wanted to know how I felt about such an asshole. I told them that he wasn't that bad and that I understood his unhappiness at having to be somewhere he didn't want to be. I didn't see Sunny for four years, however, I knew deep inside that we were mates and I knew he respected my professionalism. When Kelly Slater could not make his slot in the fifth and final challenge, the second part of Nine Lives, I had no hesitation in inviting Sunny back for another go. He willingly came, was one of the hardest chargers, one of the easiest to work with, gave a hell of a performance, and gave me the biggest Aloha when he left."

SABOTAJ

You got to love it when a kid's dad shoots a good chunk of the footage that becomes the kid's big, epic, bio-pic. Taj Burrow was already a superstar when Sabotaj was filmed. The movie was produced by Jack McCoy, and edited by Jason Muir, but the bulk of his footage was shot by his dad Vance and Taj's close friend, Rick Jakovich. Created over the course of a year, Sabotaj hit the streets in '98 and never looked back. After winning a series of video of the year awards internationally, Sabotaj still stands up today as a brilliant demonstration of supermodern wave riding at its finest. Taj is a surfer of enormous imagination and often pics in mags don't capture the ways in which he combos moves, bursts from one mad ejection right into the next. Sabotaj shows you the big picture – the winding up, the boost, the flight, the slide, the recovery and the string of shoulder torques and hip thrusts that follow. In fact, it would make a great partner to Taj's recent how-to manual, TB's Book of Hot Surfing – Sabotaj being a live demonstration of the dissections that occur in the texts.

OCCY the occumentary

Another McCoy film. This time, Occ's amazing life – the good, the bad and the beautiful. It's easy to think of Occy and only see him carving backside and overlook all the hurdles he's leapt along the way. Occ's comeback after becoming a fat boy is the stuff of sporting legend. The fact that he's been busting it up with the best of 'em for over two decades and shows no sign of slowing down poses a serious threat to any theories about surfing being a young man's sport.

PICKLED

Imagine you're knockin' 'em back at a bar in the Caribbean with the Billabong boys when all of a sudden you wake up and find yourself lost at sea in a small dinghy with only a jar of dill pickles to feed your hunger. If you imagine that your heat and starvation hallucinations might include Shane Dorian, Donavon Frankenreiter, Benji Weatherly, Rasta, Parko, Luke and Occy surfing like madmen in exotic spots the world over, then you're right in tune with Rob Wells, aka "Toons" who stars in Pickled, a boat trip of a different kind. Directed by Jamie Mosberg, Pickled takes the piss, or rather the pickle, out of serious surf films. But then there's nothing funny about the surfing, especially when it all comes to a crashing crescendo that involves huge North Point and tiny, white-suited men at the end.

THE BLUE HORIZON (Release date, January 2004)

Jack McCoy explains the motive behind his latest epic, Blue Horizon, starring world champ Andy Irons and Australian freesurfer Dave Rastovich: "Growing up here in Hawaii, I was totally immersed in surfing and I was able to watch the sport at its commercial birth – early '60s as a kid through to today. I don't think 95 percent of the surfing public understands much about our historical past. To understand where we're going we need to know where we've been. The surfing tree that branches out is full of amazing people and places that have created the sport we now know. Blue Horizon is a story of two paths, yet one epic journey, from surfing's ancient roots and on into the future with Andy and Dave."

RAIM.

RAIMANA VAN BASTOLAER SAYS: "Being born and raised in Tahiti, basically in the water, it's hard for me to imagine a life without surfing. Sometimes though, let's say it's Tuesday morning and I'm in the lineup with my friends, the sun, the fun surf, little fishes, well I give a thought to all the office workers and I'm thankful. Surfing to me is not just a "sport". Surfing is a community, a personal way of expression, a focal point for travelling, organising your life around it. It's a lifestyle, a sort of structure for every surfer, from the beginners just getting hooked, to the pros earning a living at it. In a world where all the lines of values and priorities are blurred, surfing is a solid canvas to create your life; it could be a good backbone to any lost souls of this world. Just like life itself, surfing is not easy, it's beautiful and if you can keep it simple, it's an interesting way to define yourself."

PHOTO BY TIM MCKENNA

MAR

MARGO SAYS: "At the end of the day, I surf because I love it. If I wasn't who I am, Margo this freesurfing dude, I'd still get up and surf every morning before work. It's everything, it's some-thing you can never get sick of. It frees you, it exposes you to the elements. And I love surfing by myself. That feeling of aloneness and vulnerability, that there could be a shark out there, it concen-trate the moment and gives you this tremendous feeling of being alive..."

PHOTO BY AARON LOYD

SHAUN CANSDELL SAYS: "Out there, something like 90 nautical miles from Sumatra, you can't help but reflect upon the fact that if you surf, you are very, very lucky. It really is the best feeling in the world. I sit out the back between sets and marvel at everything – the waves, the barrels, the colourful fish darting in and out of reef crevices. It's true that surfing's an escape but it's not an escape from reality – it's an escape into a fresh, cleaner world."

PHOTO BY JASON CHILDS

DON
NLE

DONAVON FRANKENREITER SAYS: "Man, it's
all about those little moments, those little
tweaks. It may not be the longest or the
most perfect wave, but something will
happen and everything will slow down. You'll
catch the reflection of the sun out of the lip,
you'll become acutely aware of the offshore
grooming the face of the wave. It might take
a second, but for that one second your
senses are amplified. Everyone who surfs
has those moments. One second. All a
dream. But it's a real-life dream."

PHOTO BY NAKI

BILLABONG TEAMRIDERS
2003 - 2004

ARGENTINA
(SURF)
NAHUEL AMALFITANO
NICOLAS AMALFITANO
ALEJO MARTINEZ

(SNOW)
EZEQUIEL HURRAIZ

AUSTRALIA
(SURF)
DINO ADRIAN
ROHAN ANNESLEY
DANIEL ASMUS
JESSICA ATKINSON
DAVE BALLARD (BODYBOARDER)
BRETT BANNISTER
DEREK BASSED
LAYNE BEACHLEY
CHRIS BENNETTS
DEAN BERTSOS
WENDY BOTHA-TODD
DEAN BOWEN
KEIGHLEY BREMNER
CHRIS BROOKS
ADRIAN BUCHAN
JESSE BUCHAN
ISSAC BUCKLEY
BRETT BURCHER
AINSLEE BURT
TAJ BURROW
ANDREW CAMPBELL
LUKE CAMPBELL
RYAN CAMPBELL
STUART CAMPBELL
SHAUN CANSDELL
LIZ CANTOR
MATT CAPEL
ALEX CARRASCO
ASHLEY CHEADLE
LUKE CHEADLE
BARRY CHENHALL
TARA CHRISTIE
JOHN CLEARY
AMANDA CLEGG
JEREMY COHEN
BEN COLLIER
ANGUS COOK
JODIE COOPER
VETEA "POTO" DAVID
JOHN DAVIES
BEAU DAY (BODYBOARDER)
DAVID DELROY-CARR
FELIX DICKENSON
PHILIPPE DIDELOT

LUKE DORRINGTON
BEDE DURBIDGE
DANE DURBIN
PETER DERHAM
LUKE EGAN
MICHAEL EPPELSTUN (BODYBOARDER)
ELLIS ERICSSON
CURTIS EWING
SHANE FELSINGER
WYLIE FOWLER
COREY GARCIA
CHRIS GERARD
WADE GOODALL
TODD GOUDIE
KOBI GRAHAM
NICK GREGORY
LUCAS GRESHAM
CALE GRIGSON
CHRISTO HALL
GLENN HALL
MITCHELL HALL (BODYBOARDER)
RYAN HARDY (BODYBOARDER)
JOSH HARRINGTON
TIM HAWKEN
DAMIEN HODGE
MICHAEL HOPKINS
MATTHEW HOWARD
PETER HUGHES
RENEE HYMAN
DEAN IEZZI
LUKE JEFFREY
JOE JORDANOFF (BODYBOARDER)
HEATH JOSKE
SAGE JOSKE
BILLY KEAN

BRAD KING
MATT LACKEY (BODYBOARDER)
DANIEL LANG
JAMIE LAMBERT
BRAD LANCASTER
AUSTIN LANGRIDGE
BRENDIN LECKIE
JOSH LEE
JUSTIN LEE
KIRA LLEWELLYN (BODYBOARDER)
ANDREW LESTER (BODYBOARDER)
SEBASTIAN LOADER
JOSH LOCK
DYLAN LONGBOTTOM
DARREN MAGEE
BRENDEN MARGIESON
LAURINA McGRATH
JOE McGREGOR
LAUREN McGREGOR

JOHN McLEAN
SIMON McSHANE
KEENAN MORGAN
LUKE NORTHY
LYNDSAY NOYES
MARK OCCHILUPO
REBECCA OAKLEY
SAM PAGE
JOEL PARKINSON
BRENT POWER
DAVID RASTOVICH
MITCHELL RAWLINS
LARA READINGS
LUKE ROBINSON
CHRISTIAN ROGULSKYJ
KABEL ROWLINSON
MEREDYTH SAUNDERS
NICK SAUNDERS (BODYBOARDER)
SHERIDIAN SHIELDS
JOSH SLABB
RHYS SMITH
STEVE SMITH
RUSSELL SPECHT
JASON STEVENSON
MADE SUDANA
CAMERON TAYLOR
PATCHULA THOMPSON
TROY THORTON
LAURIE TOWNER
NICHOLAS VASICEK
KEELAN VEITCH
BEAU WALKER
JESSE WILLIAMS
MADISON WILLIAMS
ROBERT WINTER
REBECCA WOODS
PAUL WORBOYS
DOUG YOUNG

(SKATE)
SALLY AFFLECK
CHAD BARTIE
BART CARNES
SHANE CROSS
RUSSELL GRUNDY
JOHN LORCAN
ANTHONY MACQUIRE
RENTON MILLER
BEN PAPPAS

(SNOW)
CLINT ALLAN
JAMIE ALLAN
TONY GRAHAM

NICK GREGORY
LYNDA WHITTAKER
STEVE WHITTAKER
MANDY WOOD

(BMX)
JAMIE GREY

BRAZIL
(SURF)
NATHAN BRANDI
DANILO COSTA
ELISA COSTA
CLAUDIA GONÇALVES
PEDRO HENRIQUE
CELSO JUNIOR
BRUNO MOREIRA
BRUNA SHIMIDTZ
WLADIMIR VOVÔ
RICARDO WENDHAUSEN
MARINA WERNECK

(SKATE)
LAURA ALLI
KELVIN KOEFLER
MARCELO KOSAKE
CAIO PASTEL
CÉSAR PASTEL

CANADA
(SNOW)
ALEX AUCHU
ANNIE BOULANGER
RUBE GOLDBERG
JONAS GUINN
BENJI RITCHIE
KALE STEPHENS
CHRIS TURPIN (FREE SKIER)
WARREN WILLIAMS

(SKATE)
JOE BUFFALO
WILLIAM CHRISTOFARO
JESSE LANDEN
SHELDON "SWELL" LLOYDSMITH
JESSIE VAN ROECHOUDT

(WAKE)
JF GOSSELIN
CHRIS GUARD
KEVIN HENSHAW
CHAD SHARPE

EUROPE
(SURF)
THOMAS BADY
SAM CARRIER
HODEI COLLAZO

GORDON FONTAIN
SCOTT FONTAIN
YANN FONTAIN
IKER FUENTES
DANI GARCIA
FABRICE GELEZ
NATHAN HELE
ROMAIN LAULHE
DAMIEN PRISK (BODYBOARDER)
BENJAMIN SANCHIS
CARWYN WILLIAMS

(SKATE)
EMILIO ARNANZ
TERENCE BOUGDOUR
ALI CAIRNS
KARIM CHERIF
CHRIS OLIVER
JOCKE OLSSON
PAUL SHEIR

(SNOW)
YANNICK AMAVET
ANTTI AUTTI
THOMAS EBERHARTER
JONAS EMERY
BEN KILNER
JENNY JONES
RISTO MATILLA
FLO MAUSSER
WOLLE NYVELT
MARIUS OTTERSTAD
AXEL PAUPORTE
JAMIE PHILLP

(WIND)
JOSH ANGULO

INDONESIA
(SURF)
DARMAWAN
KOMANG-KOMING
KOMBONG
MADE LANA
WYAN "BUKIT" MEI
RADITYA
RAH TU SUARGITA
WAYAN "KOPLING" WIRTAMA

(SKATE)
AGUNG KURNIAWAN (GUNG DE)
TONY SERUNTUL

(WIND)
KOMANG "BANGLI" SUARTANA
WAYAN WIRANTA

MUSIC
PADI GROUP

JAPAN
(SURF)
SHINPEI HORIGUCHI
SATOSHI KURISU
HIDETOSHI KIRITSUME
NARUMI KITAGAWA
MINORU MATSUDA (BODYBOARDER)
TOSHIHIDE MAYAGTUCHI
KEIJI MURATA
HIROTO NISHIDA

CHIGUSA NISHIYAMA (BODYBOARDER)
NORIMASA OHNO
KAZUYA SATO
HIDEYOSHI TANAKA
KYOHEI YAMADA
YESCO

NEW ZEALAND
(SURF)
NICK BLACK
FELIX DICKSON
JOHNNY FENTON
LUKE HUGHES
BEN KENNINGS
JOS KENNINGS
OWEN McMILLAN
CHRIS MILLET
JAMIE PATTERN
JAMIE PORTER
MATT SCORRINGE
BLAIR STEWART
SAM WILLIS

(SNOW)
PATRICK NEPIA
CROSBY WEBB

SOUTH AFRICA
(SURF)
RICKY BASNETT
ROBYN BASSNET
BRAD BICKNELL
ANDREW CARTER
TARRYN CHUDLEIGH
GREG EMSLIE
DAMIEN FAHRENFORT
ADRIAN GOUWS
SEAN HOLMES
GALEN HOSSACK
TARA HOSSACK
SHAUN JOUBERT
GREG LAZARUS

TAMMY LEE SMITH
LYLE MEEK
WANDA MEYER
BRAD MOMMSEN
RUDY PALMBOOM JNR
RUDY PALMBOOM SNR
SHAUN PAYNE
GERARD DU PLESSIS
JORDIE SMITH
DALE STAPLES
KLEE STRACHAN
CHAD DU TOIT
WARWICH WRIGHT
(SKATE)
STUART BRADBURN (DOWNHILL)

ADRIAN DAY
CHRISTIE WIENHAHN
(SNOW)
MARTA JECKOT
AXCEL ZANDER
(WAKE)
ROSS ASTRUP
NICK BURTON MOORE
(MOTOCROSS)
RYAN NEWTON

PERU
ROMINA ATANASOWSKY
PIERO DELUCCHI
NICOLLE FIEDLER
DANIEL FOLKMANES
ANALI GOMEZ
IAN GUBBINS
ALESSANDRA KOENIG
GIA MACAGNO
LEIA MACAGNO
BRISSA MALAGA

ALONSO MOSCOSO
MATIAS MULANOVICH
MICAELA PIQUERAS
JAVIER SWAYNE
MAGOO DE LA ROSA

USA
(SURF)
CONNIE ARIAS
RYAH ARTHUR
ANASTASIA ASHLEY
RYAN AUGENSTEIN
TORY BARRON
TONINO BENSON
ALANA BRENNAN
RYAN BRIGGS

BELEN CONNELLY
LEAH DAWSON
WESLEY DESOUZA
DONAVON FRANKENREITER
BUD FRIETAS
JULIE GONZALEZ
LEILANI GRYDE
SAM HAMMER
BRYAN HEWITSON
MARK HOLDER
ASHLEY HUNTER
LANI HUNTER
ANDY IRONS
DANIEL JONES
CALEB JOHNSTON
JEREMY JOHNSTON

KEALA KENNELLY
KYLE KENNELLY
ALEX KING
SANOE LAKE
ALBEE LAYER
DARIUES LEGG
RAVEN LUNDY
SCHUYLER McFERRAN
PETER MENDIA
MOLLI MILLER
DREW MOYE
TOMMY O'BRIEN
DANNY NICHOLS
BRIAN PACHECO
MIKE PARSONS
KELLY POTTS
RUSH RANDLE
RORY REEP
LUCAS ROGERS
COLLIN SCHILDHAUER
JASON SHIBATA
CHRIS SLAYTER
SLYDOG
HUEY SODERQUIST
STERLING SPENCER
CHE STANG
JAMIE STERLING
GAVIN SUTHERLAND
SHANE UPCHURCH
LISBETH VINDAS DIAS
GRAHAM WADE

IAN WALSH
PHILLIP WATTERS
BENJI WEATHERLY
MATT WETMORE
JUSTIN WIEGAND
SARA WILLIS

NATHAN YEOMANS
LESLIE BURSIAN,
TOMMY BURSIAN (PUERTO RICO)
RAIMANA VAN BASTOLAER (TAHITI)

(SNOW)
JUSTIN BRINK
JOHN CENTI
ANDREW CRAWFORD
TARA DAKIDES
LAUREN FOSTER
KEVIN JONES
NICK LARSON
SCOTT LEGO
AJ LIVINGSTON
VICTOR LOWRANCE
NATE ODIO
SHANE POSPISILL
TREVOR POSPISILL
MARY PRICE
BENJI RITCHIE
DAVID SCAFFIDI
RORY SILVA (FREE SKIER)
MATT STERBENZ (FREE SKIER)
JESSE UTTECH
ELIJAH VALENCIA
KURT WASTELL

(SKATE)
DEVIN BRANKOVICH
BEN CABREANA
QUIM CARDONA
KURTIS COLAMONICO
BEN GORE
DANIEL HANEY
TYLER HANSON

WILL HARMON
RODNEY JONES
CHRIS KENDALL
DEVON LAMB
BUCKEY LASEK
RICKY LAVATO
ALIKI LEE
DEVIN LYNN
JEFFREY MARSHELL
JAMES McKNIGHT
STEVE NARDONE
BRIAN PATCH
MIKE PETERSON
DAVID ROSE
WILLY SANTOS

TAYLOR SMITH
BRETT SOREM
JESSIE VAN ROECHOUDT

(WAKE)
BUSTER CARTWRIGHT
BRIAN GRUBB
COLLIN WRIGHT
LAUREN LOE
BUSTER LUTGERT
DANNY HARF (WETSUITS ONLY)

(BMX)
RICK THORNE

(KITE)
CHRIS GILBERT
JULIE GILBERT

HONCHOS

150

NAME: DEREK O'NEILL
POSITION: GLOBAL CEO
JOINED COMPANY: 1989
RELEVANT FACTS: FOUNDER OF EUROPE OPERATION.
SURFER/SNOWBOARDER

NAME: GARY PEMBERTON
POSITION: CHAIRMAN OF THE BOARD
JOINED COMPANY: 1999
RELEVANT FACTS: BUSINESS GURU!

NAME: SHAYNE PALFREYMAN
POSITION: GLOBAL CFO
JOINED COMPANY: 1999
RELEVANT FACTS: HOLDER OF CHEQUE BOOK

AUSTRALASIA
NEW ZEALAND

NAME: NILAN FONSEKA
POSITION: GENERAL MANAGER
JOINED COMPANY: 1990
RELEVANT FACTS: QUIET ACHIEVER

NAME: GRAHAM WIGG
POSITION: MENS SALES MANAGER FOR BILLABONG
JOINED COMPANY: 1991
RELEVANT FACTS: FORMER AUCKLAND SURF CHAMPION

NAME: SCOTT CASEY
POSITION: BRAND MANAGER
JOINED COMPANY: 1995
RELEVANT FACTS: FORMER MEMBER OF NZ SCHOOL
BOYS SURFING TEAM

NAME: SONIA STEVENSON
POSITION: GIRLS SALES MANAGER FOR BILLABONG
JOINED COMPANY: 1991
RELEVANT FACTS: NEW ZEALAND JUNIOR SURFING
TEAM COACH 1996-97

JAPAN

NAME: IETOSHI UEDA
POSITION: CEO GSM JAPAN
JOINED COMPANY: 2000
RELEVANT FACTS: STILL RIPS

INDONESIA

NAME: PAUL ANDERSON
POSITION: GENERAL MANAGER
JOINED COMPANY: 2000
RELEVANT FACTS: FORMER AUSTRALIAN
LONGBOARD CHAMPION

MALAYSIA/SINGPORE

NAME: JOHN INNUS
POSITION: MANAGING DIRECTOR
JOINED COMPANY: 1990
RELEVANT FACTS: MALAYSIAN WAVE POOL
MASTER

HONG KONG

NAME: RICKY CHAN
POSITION: ADMINISTRATION MANAGER
JOINED COMPANY: 2000
RELEVANT FACTS: KING OF GARMENTS

AUSTRALIA

NAME: DOUGALL WALKER
POSITION: GENERAL MANAGER OF AUSTRALIA
JOINED COMPANY: 1986
RELEVANT FACTS: BILLABONG PATRIOT

NAME: PETER CASEY
POSITION: GLOBAL PRODUCT MANAGER
JOINED COMPANY: 1984
RELEVANT FACTS: MASTER OF DETAIL

NAME: SHANNAN NORTH
POSITION: NATIONAL SALES MANAGER
JOINED COMPANY: 1993
RELEVANT FACTS: MONGREL SURF DOG

NAME: ANDREW FLITTON
POSITION: NATIONAL BRAND MANAGER
JOINED COMPANY: 1989
RELEVANT FACTS: SURF VISIONARY

NAME: HEIDI BARTHOLOMEW
POSITION: GIRLS BRAND MANAGER
JOINED COMPANY: 1992
RELEVANT FACTS: FROM THE WORLD-FAMOUS GOLD
COAST BARTHOLOMEW FAMILY

NAME: MARK HENDERSON
POSITION: MENS PRODUCT DEVELOPMENT MANAGER
JOINED COMPANY: 1992
RELEVANT FACTS: FORMER WANDERING SURF ADVENTURER
WITH AN EYE FOR DETAIL

NAME: FELICITY AVAKIEN
POSITION: ACCESSORIES PRODUCT DEVELOPMENT MANAGER
JOINED COMPANY: 1995
RELEVANT FACTS: MASTER OF HER TRADE

NAME: TINA SCOTT
POSITION: HUMAN RELATIONS
JOINED COMPANY: 1992
RELEVANT FACTS: INDISPENSABLE!!

USA

NAME: PAUL NAUDE
POSITION: PRESIDENT BILLABONG USA
JOINED COMPANY: 1998
RELEVANT FACTS: SURFER/SNOWBOARDER/DIPLOMAT

NAME: STEVE WILSON
POSITION: HEAD PRODUCT DEVELOPMENT MANAGER
JOINED COMPANY: 1999
RELEVANT FACTS: STYLE MASTER

NAME: GRAHAM STAPELBERG
POSITION: MARKETING MANAGER
JOINED COMPANY: 1998
RELEVANT FACTS: FORMER ASP PRESIDENT

NAME: MILICA PRESTON
POSITION: COO
JOINED COMPANY: 1999
RELEVANT FACTS: OPERATIONS PAR EXCELLENCE

NAME: RICHARD SANDERS
POSITION: SALES MANAGER
JOINED COMPANY: 1989
RELEVANT FACTS: SURFER/GOLFER/NICE GUY

NAME: KAREN SARVER
POSITION: VP CORPORATE AFFAIRS
JOINED COMPANY: 1998
RELEVANT FACTS: THE UNOFFICIAL BOSS

THE AMERICAS

NAME: FRANÇOIS CARRETE
POSITION: VP CANADA AND INTERNATIONAL SALES
JOINED COMPANY: 1996
RELEVANT FACTS: BASQUE CONFORMING AMERICAN
ON THE WANTED LIST

NAME: MARK MACHADO
POSITION: VP OUTERWEAR AND ACCESSORIES
JOINED COMPANY: 1992
RELEVANT FACTS: SURFER/SNOWBOARDER/
INVENTOR

NAME: TOM GUMPERT
POSITION: VP FINANCE
JOINED COMPANY: 2000
RELEVANT FACTS: IT'S CELTIC SOUNDS OR NOTHING

NAME: STEVE CULLEY
POSITION: VP RETAIL OPERATIONS
JOINED COMPANY: 2001
RELEVANT FACTS: JOHN ELWAY WANNABE

NAME: JOE LONG
POSITION: VP PRODUCTION
JOINED COMPANY: 1998
RELEVANT FACTS: SMOOTH OPERATOR

NAME: JON HEINDEL
POSITION: VP INFORMATION TECHNOLOGY
JOINED COMPANY: 1998
RELEVANT FACTS: HUGE GREEN BAY PACKER FAN

OTHER SENIOR MANAGEMENT INCLUDE ROB McCARTY,
CATHY PAIK, ROB WILLIS, ANGIE BROBERG, CANDY HARRIS,
ENICH HARRIS, ANNE MACHADO, PEDRO PEREZ AND
ANGIE McGRAW

EUROPE

NAME: STEPHANE WEINHOLD
POSITION: GENERAL MANAGER
JOINED COMPANY: 1997
RELEVANT FACTS: MULTILINGUAL, SNOWBOARDER/SURFER

NAME: MICHELE ALONSO
POSITION: FINANCE AND ADMINISTRATION MANAGER EUROPE
JOINED COMPANY: 1993
RELEVANT FACTS: IRON LADY OF THE EUROPEAN
SURF INDUSTRY

NAME: FRANCK GOMIS
POSITION: SALES MANAGER EUROPE
JOINED COMPANY: 1994
RELEVANT FACTS: THE FIRST EUROPEAN PRO SURFER
ON THE WORLD TOUR (1979-1984)

NAME: REID PINDER
POSITION: MARKETING MANAGER EUROPE
JOINED COMPANY: 1992
RELEVANT FACTS: KEEPER OF THE CORE

NAME: CARL WIESER
POSITION: CONTEST AND TEAM
JOINED COMPANY: 1994
RELEVANT FACTS: SURFER AND SOUL BROTHER

NAME: CRAIG SAGE
POSITION: SALES MANAGER SPAIN
JOINED COMPANY: 1987
RELEVANT FACTS: NEVER MISSES A MUNDAKA SWELL

NAME: ROBERTO PECCIOLI
POSITION: ITALIAN DISTRIBUTOR
JOINED COMPANY: 1988
RELEVANT FACTS: SMOOTHER THAN DE NIRO

NAME: PAULO MARTINS
POSITION: PORTUGAL DISTRIBUTOR
JOINED COMPANY: 1990
RELEVANT FACTS: SURFER, MAYOR OF ERICEIRA

NAME: MIGUEL FORTES
POSITION: PORTUGAL SALES MANAGER
JOINED COMPANY: 1991
RELEVANT FACTS: WINNER OF THE BILLABONG MADEIRA
BIG-WAVE CHALLENGE 1997

BRAZIL

NAME: CHRIS KYPRIOTIS
POSITION: GENERAL MANAGER
JOINED COMPANY: 2003
RELEVANT FACTS: NEW GUY ON THE BLOCK

NAME: RICARDO PIAZZA
POSITION: DIRECTOR
JOINED COMPANY: 1994
RELEVANT FACTS: LIFE OF THE PARTY

VENEZUELA

NAME: ALAN GALSKY
POSITION: GENERAL MANAGER
JOINED COMPANY: 1998
RELEVANT FACTS: MAN OF THE PEOPLE

ARGENTINA

NAME: ROY TARRAB
POSITION: GENERAL MANAGER
JOINED COMPANY: 1999
RELEVANT FACTS: LEADS BY EXAMPLE

ISRAEL

NAME: YIZHAK (TZAHI) HAUS
POSITION: GENERAL MANAGER
JOINED COMPANY: 1994
RELEVANT FACTS: ISRAEL LONGBOARD CHAMPION
(1991-1994)

SOUTH AFRICA

NAME: CHERON KRAAK
POSITION: FOUNDER AND CHIEF OF
BILLABONG SOUTH AFRICA
JOINED COMPANY: 1984
RELEVANT FACTS: QUEEN OF J-BAY

PERU/CHILE

NAME: MAX DE LA ROSA TORO
POSITION: GENERAL MANAGER
JOINED COMPANY: 1989
RELEVANT FACTS: EX PRESIDENT OF THE PERUVIAN
SURFING FEDERATION

NAME: MAGOO DE LA ROSA TORO
POSITION: EVENTS CO-ORDINATOR/PARTNER
JOINED COMPANY: 1989
RELEVANT FACTS: EIGHT TIMES PERUVIAN NATIONAL
SURFING CHAMPION